A Guide to Help Renew the Mind for
Life Transformation

LORD
HELP ME
With Me

*"My Help Comes From The LORD, Who
Made Heaven and Earth"- Psalms 121:2*

JEROME W. TERRY

A Guide to Help Renew the Mind for Life Transformation

L O R D
H e l p M e
W i t h M e

"My help comes from the LORD, Who made heaven and earth" – Psalms 121:2

J e r o m e W . T e r r y

All rights reserved. ISBN NO. **978-1-943409-89-1**

Printed in the United States of America

Pure Thoughts Publishing LLC

www.PureThoughtsPublishing.com

Dedication

•

I want to dedicate this project to a woman that I love and appreciate dearly. This project is dedicated to my lovely lady and my partner for life. This wonderful person that I am referring to is no other than my beautiful wife Racquel 'Niki' Terry.

The Bible declares, "He who finds a wife finds a good thing, And obtains favor from the LORD." (Proverbs 18:22 NKJV). When we as men find a wife, it is an indication that God's favor is on our lives. Finding a woman may not be that difficult; our challenge as men sometimes is finding the woman that God has prepared to be our wife.

When we find a wife, it is because God has favored us with vision to recognize our wife when we see her. I thank God for this woman that He has placed in my life. God's favor is truly on my life and it is evidenced by the woman He has given to me.

Racquel, I want to thank you for sticking by my side through the hard times. I want to thank you for putting up me through my struggles as a man and through the struggles of becoming what God would desire for me to be. I want to thank you for seeing the God in me and allowing me to go after God and the dream He gave me while being supportive and faithful.

You have truly been a blessing to my life. I dedicate this project to you. For the rest of my life, because of your faithfulness to me, and more importantly because of your faithfulness to God, whatever God puts into my hands is yours. I love you and I appreciate you with my whole heart.

Sincerely your husband,

Jerome

Table of Contents

Introduction

'LORD Help Me With Me' is our desperate cry to God as it relates to our necessity for transformation. It is one thing to have a desire to be transformed. It is a different thing to need to be transformed. As God walks with us, He reveals to us that transformation is not only a desire, but a necessity.

Having God in our lives is more than a desire. We do not study our Bibles, implement fast and consecrations, or even offer our requests to God just because we want to. We study our Bibles, we fast, and we pray because we have to. We need a relationship with God. It is our relationship with God, coupled with adversity, that causes us to grow and to become more like Him.

The inspiration for this book's theme comes from a song composed and sung by a legendary Gospel artist by the name of Tamela Mann. The name of that song of course, is "Change Me." If you have not had the opportunity to listen to this song, I strongly suggest, and I highly recommend that you do so before continuing to read this book.

Within our hearts, we find our motives, our intentions, and our desires. Why we do what we do and our desires lie in the heart. This song comes from the heart of an individual that praises and worships God. It also comes from the heart of an individual that has received the revelation that they are in need of a change.

God instructs and encourages us to "Delight yourself also in the LORD, And He shall give you the desires of your heart. Commit your way to the LORD, Trust also in Him, And He shall bring it to pass." (Psalm 37:4-5 NKJV). As we pursue God and make Him our delight, He will bring to fruition those desires that our legitimate; and the illegitimate ones He will either eradicate or give us the power to dominate them.

This book not only deals with the condition of the heart but primarily the condition of the mind. Long before change occurs in our conduct and conversation, change must first occur in our minds. We are only transformed into what God would have us to be by the renewing of our minds. We should learn to study our Bibles for the purpose of repairing our hearts and to change how we think.

We should learn the importance of internalizing God's Word. In the words of King David, "Your Word I have hidden in my heart, That I might not sin against You." (Psalms 119:11 NKJV). The mistake that we frequently make is to study God's Word to teach, or to preach or to share with others. We should study Scripture for the purpose of mind renewal in order to acquire the transformation that needs to take place in our own individual lives.

Paul says this to Timothy, "Be diligent to present yourself approved to God, a worker who does not need to be ashamed, rightly dividing the word of truth." (II Timothy 2:15 NKJV). The traditional, Old English, or commonly known as the King James Version of the Bible, says "study to show yourself approved." The question now becomes why are we studying Scripture? Are we studying Scripture to have the approval of people? Or are we studying Scripture to have the approval of God?

The study that God approves of is the type of study that repairs our hearts, changes how we think, and transforms our lives. What we learn through experience is that we cannot renew anyone else's mind but our own. One of Satan's biggest ploys is that he uses other people, especially those we really care about to distract us. We can use unnecessary time and energy, trying to change someone else's mind. This can be depleting and stressful.

The only mind that we are responsible for changing is our own. We should dedicate our time and energy to changing our own mind. We have a challenging enough time attempting to change our own mind let alone attempting to change someone else's mind.

When we read Scripture, we must understand that it was written for the purpose of learning how to live. Paul put it like this; "For whatever things were written before were written for our learning, that we through the patience and comfort of the Scriptures might have hope." (Romans 15:4 NKJV). The word hope here is translated as confident expectation.

God provides comfort and confident expectation in Him so that we may live our lives with patience and endurance. Bishop Noel Jones in the past has called the Bible "a book of relationships." It is a book of relationships and experiences that provides comfort and confident expectation in God as we navigate life and the process of transformation.

Transformation is challenging. For one to suggest that transformation is not challenging would suggest that that individual has not scratched the surface of the transformation process. Changing our minds is one of the most heart-wrenching things we will ever have to do. The beautiful thing about it is that God does not allow us to change our minds by ourselves. He does not do it for us, but He does however do it with us and through us.

God walks with us and He talks with us through the process of transformation. He will talk us through some things, and He will walk us through some things. He talks us out of some things, and He walks us out of some things as well.

That's why we appreciate God the way that we do. We appreciate Him so much because He loves us when oftentimes we do not have the capacity to love ourselves. He loves us even when we do not have the capacity to love Him in return.

Because of how we think, we sometimes think we are in pursuit of God. We are really not in pursuit of God. Not really. Not like we sometimes think that we are.

The truth of the matter is that He is really in pursuit of us. If God never pursued us, we would never have a desire to have a relationship with Him at all. The sole intended purpose of His pursuit is to transform us into worshipers of Him.

Jesus says this, "But the hour is coming, and now is, when the true worshipers will worship the Father in spirit and truth; for the Father is seeking such to worship Him. God is Spirit, and those who worship Him must worship in spirit and truth." (John 4:23-24 NKJV). His pursuit of us is what causes us to change our minds and transforms us into individuals that live for His glory.

God's desire for us is to bring Him glory. Our anxiety does not bring Him glory. Being fearful does not bring God glory. We bring Him glory when we are at peace with whatever state we find ourselves to be in. We bring God glory when we have joy that we cannot comprehend or explain.

True peace and real joy have a focal point. We only have the Peace of God and the Joy of the LORD when we trust God with our hearts, and when we have a mind that is focused on Him. Our focal point is our Savior and Deliver Christ Jesus, who died on a cross, rose from the dead, and lives forevermore. It is in Him whom we put our trust.

Our circumstances whether favorable or unfavorable can never bring us joy. Our situation whether good or bad can never bring us peace. Favorable circumstances can bring a temporary peace or a temporary joy which we oftentimes refer to as happiness.

To have peace that surpasses all understanding and to have joy unspeakable that is full of God's glory, we have to believe that we are never alone. We believe that we are never alone because we have received the revelation from God that we are not and will not be forsaken by Him.

Circumstances fluctuate. People come and go. But our God will never leave us, nor will He ever forsake us. He is with us until the end.

The Spirit of the living God teaches us how to separate our thoughts from our circumstances whether our circumstances are positive or negative. He strengthens our hearts with His Word by His Spirit so that we can have thoughts of peace and a heart to trust Him. We should allow God access to our heart so that we may have a mind to worship and praise Him through anything.

When we worship God and appreciate Him, we find out that the things that Satan desires to use to destroy us actually constructs our lives and builds our character. When God brings us out of our mess, we are able to decree and declare the song sung by Pastor Marvin Sapp, "I never would have made it without You. I would have lost it all; but now I see how You were there for me!"

God feeds us truth that is working in agreement with His love. God does not give us accurate information with the intent to destroy us. He has too much compassion and too much mercy to do that.

God gives us accurate information with the intention to help us, to instruct us and to correct us. God gives us accurate information to guide us, to deliver us, to save us, and to set us free. The information that God gives us always works in concert with encouragement; with the purpose of moving us to the next level in Him.

'LORD Help Me With Me'. This is our petition as children to a Father that is in love with us His people dearly. May this book bless you, your loved ones and whoever you may encounter as you commit to your journey of transformation.

Sincerely, your brother,

Jerome W. Terry

Chapter 1

Repentance Granted

"And their scribes and the Pharisees complained against His (Jesus) disciples, saying, 'Why do You eat and drink with tax collectors and sinners?' Jesus answered and said to them, 'Those who are well have no need of a physician, but those who are sick. I have not come to call the righteous, but sinners, to repentance.'" (Luke 5:30-32 NKJV).

This should be said before we move into this chapter. It has been said to us that Jesus does not hear sinners pray or that He does not talk to sinners. I would just like to say that I am so glad that this is not true. I know that God talks to sinners and that He hears sinners because He hears and talks to me. If the statement that God does not talk to sinners were true, I would not be here right now writing this book. I am only living and breathing today because God is gracious enough and merciful enough to hear my humble cry.

Todd Galberth's remake of the song "Do Not Pass Me By" is a wonderful depiction of the heart of a man who is crying out to God after finding themselves at the end of themselves. We would not be here today had He not heard our cry for deliverance. We should not receive the message that God does not hear the sinner. Why would He die for us as sinners and then decide not to hear us when we call upon Him?

The Apostle Paul says this, "This is a faithful saying and worthy of all acceptance, that Christ Jesus came into the world to save sinners, of whom I am chief." (I Timothy 1:15 NKJV). We should accept this statement for ourselves. We as individuals, should accept that we are the chief sinner in any room we step in. This acknowledgment eradicates arrogance and creates humility.

We want to have the mindset that there is no-one in the room that can out-sin us. This is self-awareness and true humility. The potential for us to be dysfunctional and destructive is un-matched by no-one. This should be our mindset.

When God gives us the victory, our mindset is; 'If God can save me, then He can save anybody. If God can deliver me, then He can deliver anyone. If He can bring me out, then He can bring anyone out of whatever they may be going through.'

Let us continue and hear what our God has to say shall we? The word repentance is a very familiar word within Christian circles. This word is used frequently and often as it relates to behavior challenges that we may be experiencing as we strive to walk with God.

When we are first introduced to Jesus, one of the first words we hear as it relates to our behavior is repentance. While we are walking with God, one of the words that we often hear as it relates to our conduct and conversation is repentance. Our immediate perception of the word repentance is to change how we behave so that we can walk with God. Our first inclination as we attempt to apply repentance to our lives is to eliminate the conduct and/or conversation that displeases God so that we can have eternal life.

For years we have attempted to 'repent' to no avail. We have tried to change our behavior. LORD knows that we have tried. We have tried to stop doing some of the things that we enjoy doing in order to have a relationship with God. We have attempted to please God by changing our behavior, and we have gained frustrated through this lack of success. Our lack of success has stemmed from how we have interpreted the word repentance or allowed others to interpret the word repentance for us.

Does God desire for us to walk with Him this way? Does He expect for us to live our lives focusing all of our energy and efforts on eliminating all the things in our lives that we enjoy, just so we can make sure we make it to heaven?

On top of all that, the people in our lives are telling us that we need to 'repent.' They have grown frustrated and impatient with us because they find our conduct and/or conversation to be egregious and offensive. LORD, help us to understand.

Maybe we need to take another look at the word repentance and find out what God is saying about it. According to the Greeks, metanoia, the word often used for repentance in the Bible literally means a changing of one's mind. As it relates to repentance, what God desires for us to do is to change our thinking.

What we begin to learn and discover as we begin to mature in God is that when we change our minds, then God will change our lives. God is not coming after us in order to attack or address our behavior initially. God is coming after us with His Love, to arrest our hearts, so that we through His Word can conquer our thoughts. When we think like Him, we live like Him.

We learn through life experiences to give God our hearts. God has to have access to the heart in order to control our thoughts through His Word. God's Word must be hidden in the heart for Him to do what we need Him to do in our lives. When God's Word is absence from the heart, then our carnality will control how we think.

There is a difference between having His Word hidden in the head and having His Word hidden in the heart. Scripture can be memorized without being internalized. Allowing God access to the heart is to internalize His Word which will alter how we think and produce a life that glorifies Him.

Allowing God access to the heart is not something that is done on a one-time basis. Allowing God access to the heart is not something that is done annually. It is not something that is done monthly or weekly. Allowing God access to the heart is something that is done daily. Fellowship with God is a daily necessity.

We should allow God access to the heart. The mind does not control the heart. The heart controls the mind. How we think is contingent upon what is in the heart. How we live is dependent upon how we think.

When we receive the revelation that how we live has to change, then we will partner with God in our mind renewal process. When we receive the revelation that life transformation requires mind renewal, we will allow God to regulate the heart with His Love. Why? Because, "For as he (man) thinks in his heart, so is he" (Proverbs 23:7a NKJV).

The reason why we have grown so frustrated and so discouraged is because we were taking an external approach to our own deliverance. What we discover is that God does not change us externally even if the individuals in our lives or the individuals around our lives attempt to change us by taking this approach. The mistake we make and the mistake others make while handling us is attempting to change us from an external vantage point or an external point-of-view. Behavior does not tell the entire story.

People's perception of us will be incomplete when they do not have the compassion to look inside of our spirits. God is omniscient and full of mercy and His compassion never fails; so His perception of us is complete. He takes into account what we have had to endure while He is molding us and shaping us. For some odd reason, the people in our lives and the people around our lives often have a tendency of being incapable of doing this.

When we are ready for change, we take a look at our behavior, which is clear and evident that it displeases God. We compare our behavior to God's Word and see that our behavior is in direct opposition to Him. What we have a tendency to do is to eradicate the behavior so that we can please Him. The results are typically not long-term because we address the behavior without addressing the mind.

A perfect example of this is when one attempts to try to quit using products that contain nicotine. There are some people that find the use of nicotine products highly offensive. After all, nicotine products, depending on how they are used, are not only harmful to the person using them but also can be harmful to the individuals around the individual using them.

In my personal life I have wrestled with nicotine addiction and I have attempted to quit. I attempted to quit by throwing the nicotine products in the trash only later to find myself digging them out of the trash. I was attempting to change my behavior without changing my thinking.

God is so good because he does not handle us the same way as others do. God does not even handle us the same way we handle ourselves. When God comes after us, He comes after us to arrest our hearts so we can be empowered by His grace and mercy to change our minds.

When we change our minds, by being empowered by His Spirit and the Truth of His Word in us, then our behavior will follow; because the mind does not follow behavior, behavior always follows the mind. A mind change that is connected to a heart that appreciates God, respects Him, and that is in love with Him will ultimately produce a life-style change.

Our behavior is a representation of our thoughts and a reflection of the meditation of the heart. "The heart is deceitful above all things, and desperately wicked: who can know it?" (Jeremiah 17:9 KJV). When God takes inventory of our lives, He does it from an internal vantage point or an internal point-of-view.

For God to have full access to our lives, we must come into agreement with Him about what He sees in our heart and what He sees in our thoughts. "And there is no creature hidden from His sight, but all things are naked and open to the eyes of Him to whom we must give account." (Hebrews 4:13 NKJV).

It is critical that we agree with God with what He sees in us. In order for us to be transformed, we have to agree with God. We must not allow fear to cause us to disagree with Him. We must not allow the condemnatory thoughts that we have towards ourselves to cause us to disagree with Him.

Sometimes we disagree with God and we are not as transparent with Him as we should be because we believe that He is condemning us. When we are afraid of God, we do not trust Him. We disagree with God because it is very difficult to be transparent with someone who we do not trust.

I have good news for you. God is not condemning us. He is saving us. There is a significant distinction. When we condemn, we destroy. When we save, we build. Because God is good, and because He is saving us, and because He is building us, He can be trusted.

"For God so loved the world that He gave His only begotten Son, that whoever believes in Him should not perish but have everlasting life." (John 3:16 NKJV). This is a very popular Scripture and very well recognized. I may even like the next one better. "For God did not send His Son into the world to condemn the world, but that the world through Him might be saved." (John 3:17 NKJV).

We should always remember that God loves us and is saving us. Organized religion, the traditions of men, denomination, and the personal agenda of "wolves in sheep's clothing" have taught us that we should be intimidated, terrified, or even frighten by God. Satan desires for us to be intimidated by God so that we are too afraid to approach Him.

Religion, denomination and the traditions of men has taught us that we should be petrified of God. We should respect God, or we should revere Him, but we should never be afraid of Him. Relationship and fellowship with the Savior teaches us that God is merciful enough and compassionate enough to be trusted. "Oh, taste and see that the LORD is good; Blessed is the man who trusts in Him!" (Psalms 34:8 NKJV).

Sometimes we are blinded and not fully able to see what is in our hearts. This blindness can be caused by pride when the manifestation of behavior is not present. Just because we do not see the evil in our hearts, which we typically only identify by misconduct, does not mean our heart is not deceitful and desperately wicked.

It is quite possible that the evil that is in our hearts is not manifesting itself not because it does not exist; it is not manifesting itself only because of a lack of opportunity. When opportunity presents itself, the evil that is in our hearts, the evil that only God can see will manifest itself every-time though how we behave.

That's why we shouldn't brag on how "holy" we think we are. We shouldn't think more highly ourselves than we ought to. When opportunity presents itself, we find out that we are not as "holy", or as "saved" as we think.

David said, "I will bless the LORD at all times and; His praise shall continually be in my mouth." (Psalms 34:1 NKJV). We praise God because He is good not because we are good.

We bless The LORD at all times because, "It is of the LORD's mercies that we are not consumed because his compassions fail not. They are new every morning: great is Thy faithfulness." (Lamentations 3:22, 23 KJV).

We praise Him through the good times and through the bad times because His faithfulness is so great. We praise Him and bless Him at all times because "Surely goodness and mercy shall follow me all the days of my life: and I will dwell in the house of the LORD forever." (Psalms 23:6 KJV).

Jeremiah said, "Who can know it?" (Jeremiah 17:9b KJV); when referring to the heart. This is the Word that we should come into agreement with God about. We should agree with God that we cannot know our own heart. Only God can know it. When we allow this Word to be established in our heart and in our thoughts, it will keep us humble and always have us in a position for God to reveal Himself to us.

We need God's Word to change us internally. We need a spiritual heart transplant or in other words we need heart repair. We also need a mind change. We need God's Word to define us. God says this. "For I know the thoughts that I think toward you, says the LORD, thoughts of peace and not of evil, to give you a future and a hope." (Jeremiah 29:11 NKJV).

Oftentimes we think negatively of ourselves because we have defined ourselves by our behavior. We also define ourselves by the opinions of others because they have defined us by what they see externally. When we do this we are making a terrible mistake.

The thoughts of others towards us may be negative. The thoughts of others towards us may be hostile. Our thoughts even towards ourselves may be negative and hostile because of our behavior and because of everything in our lives that we have had to endure. But those thoughts are not the thoughts of God towards us.

The thoughts of God towards us are not negative. The thoughts of God towards us are not evil. The thoughts of God towards us are good. The thoughts of God towards us are thoughts of peace. His plan is for us to live our lives with expectation and to have continual fellowship with Him.

When God says He has thoughts of peace towards us what He is saying is that He has thoughts of reconciliation towards us. God is not thinking about condemning us. He is thinking about reconciling us to Him. God's Word does not come to push us farther away from Him. God's Word always comes to draw us closer to Him.

The question now becomes why have we given so much significance to the thoughts of people? Why do we care so much about what people think about us? Sometimes we become individuals who make changes to our lives because we are seeking the approval or validation of other people. We should never make changes to our lives to gain the approval of people. We should never make changes to our lives because we are seeking validation from someone who is in our lives temporarily.

Sometimes the people we change for leave our lives involuntarily. Sometimes the people we make changes for leave our lives voluntarily. As a result, we lose our motivation for transformation. We should only make changes to our lives for the approval of the only two relationships that we have, which are eternal. When we make changes to our lives, we should only make them for God, and we also should make them for ourselves. The only two eternal relationships that we have are God and self.

When the people in our lives or when the people around our lives decide that they would like to be a part of our lives, then they will ultimately benefit from the transformation that takes place in our lives. When the people in our lives or when the people around our lives leave our lives involuntarily through death, then may the

LORD help us to grief properly so that we may move forward with the rest of our lives.

When the people in our lives or when the people around our lives leave our lives voluntarily through their decision, then may the LORD help us to grief properly so that we may move forward with the rest of our lives. We should always make changes to our lives for God's approval because He will never leave us nor forsake us. He is the only one that will never leave us or never give up on us; so because of that we should never give up on ourselves.

We should also only make the type of changes to our lives that God would like for us to make. Changes that will bring glory to Him and for the benefit of self. Why? I'm so glad you asked. Until we learn how to care for self properly, we can never care for someone else properly.

We cannot be good to anyone until we are first good to ourselves. When we love God, we are good to self. When we receive God's forgiveness, we forgive ourselves. We love God when we receive the revelation that He first loves us.

God loves us first. Our love for Him is initiated by His love for us. It is God's love for us which empowers us to love self and to love our neighbor as we love ourselves.

There is no one in our lives that can love us the way Jesus loves us. It is going to take a whole lot of love, a whole lot of compassion, and a whole lot of patience to change us. The only one with enough love to transform us is God. We should always make changes to our lives for God's glory and for our own benefit. When God is helping us to make necessary changes to our lives, then the people in our lives and the people around our lives will ultimately benefit as well from our transformation.

Our spouses will benefit. Our children will benefit. Our parents will benefit. Our siblings will benefit. Our friends will benefit. Our enemies will even benefit from our transformation.

We have to admit to ourselves that the thoughts of others towards us may never change. This refers to the people that we genuinely care about and the people we could care less about. We have to admit to ourselves that we cannot live our lives trying to please people. We also have to admit to ourselves that we cannot live our lives trying to change people.

The thoughts of others towards us may continue to be negative. The thoughts of others are revealed by their words. "For out of the abundance of the heart the mouth speaks." (Matthew 12:34b NKJV). We can choose to define ourselves by the thoughts of men, women, boys and girls. We can also choose to define ourselves by the thoughts of God. We choose the latter.

Repentance Granted Part II

The thoughts that God thinks towards us are good. God loves us in spite of our past. God loves us in spite of our present circumstances or current situation. We might have adverse circumstances, and we may be in a situation that we really don't want to be in but we are loved by God.

Even when the people in our lives and the people around our lives do not love us, we are loved by God. God is patient with us when others are not. God is long-suffering towards us when others are ready to turn their back on us and walk away.

Our mother and our earthly father may not love us. Our spouses may turn their backs on us. Our own children might not even want a relationship with us. Our family may not have anything to do with us, but God always desires a relationship with us. "When my father and my mother forsake me, then the LORD will take me up." (Psalms 27:10 KJV).

The people in our lives may not be able to handle us, but God can always handle us. He has enough grace to handle us. God has enough mercy to hold us. The blood that He shed on a cross called Calvary is powerful enough.

An old familiar gospel song composed and song by Andrae Crouch says this; "It reaches to the highest mountain, it flows to the lowest valley, the blood that gives me strength, from day to day, it will never, ever, lose its power!"

The blood of Jesus will never lose its power! His blood will never lose its power because it is validated by His own resurrection! Jesus's blood will never lose its power because He rose from the dead and is alive forevermore. We do not have to be on the mountain to communicate with God. I don't care what valley we may find ourselves in, we can always call upon Him.

"Let us, therefore, come boldly unto the throne of grace, that we may obtain mercy, and find grace to help in time of need." (Hebrews 4:16 KJV). We are not approaching a throne of judgement. We are approaching a throne of grace. We go to the throne of grace, so we can find forgiveness and strength to overcome what we are wrestling with in our personal lives.

We go to God to ask Him to forgive us, and we ask Him to help us. Our prayer is, 'Father forgive me! Forgive me, LORD! Forgive me!' And, 'Father help me! Help me LORD! Help me!' God's mercy releases us from guilt and condemnation. His grace empowers us to overcome our personal difficulties.

When we attempt to rationalize or justify our dysfunction, we become un-repentant. On-the-hand, when we acknowledge it, or when we come into agreement with God about it, He will forgive us and deliver us from it. "If we confess our sins, He is faithful and just to forgive us our sins and to cleanse us from all unrighteousness." (I John 1:9 NKJV). God says, 'repentance granted'.

It is very well possible that there are people in our lives or around our lives who we are unable to be transparent with. Sometimes people despise us or reject us when we are transparent with them about what's wrong with us. Sometimes people see our contrition and our remorse and use it as opportunity to exploit us or manipulate us because we feel guilty over the mistakes that we have made.

I am so glad that God is not like people. People may despise us when we are genuinely contrite and remorseful; but a remorseful spirit and a contrite heart God will never despise. "The sacrifices of God are a broken spirit, A broken and a contrite heart – These, O God, you will not despise." (Psalms 51:17 NKJV). I am so glad that God will never despise our contrition or our remorse.

We should receive God's Word daily so He can change our thoughts. We need God's Word to change how we see Him and how we see our circumstances. We also need God's Word to change how we see others and most importantly how we see ourselves.

When God is calling us to repent, He is calling us to change our thinking. It is not something that is negative at all. It is actually something that is beautiful and positive. We sometimes see it as a negative because we have toxic relationships that we think we need; or we have destructive things in our lives that we are not ready to release into His hands.

Repentance is challenging. Changing the mind is challenging because we are being asked to change something that we really do not want to change. We are being asked to change our minds about becoming less dependent on the things of this world and more dependent on Him. We are being asked to become independent of something or of someone we think we need. We are being asked to become independent from something or someone that we enjoy; but at the same time is destroying us and those around us.

We should not focus our repentance or our mind change on the thing or the person that we are becoming independent from. We should always focus our repentance or mind change on our God; the one that we are becoming dependent on. We repent or change our minds about God; our Heavenly Father who is full of mercy and compassion through our LORD and Savior Christ Jesus.

Jesus is our compassionate physician who can be trusted. Jesus is our surgeon. Surgeries require submission. Jesus has to have our consent to perform surgery on us. "Submit yourselves therefore to God. Resist the devil, and he will flee from you." (James 4:7 KJV). When we submit to our merciful and compassionate Heavenly Father, He empowers us with grace and mercy to resist any temptation that Satan throws our way.

God is sitting on a 'Throne of Grace'. He is always ready to receive us with mercy to free us from the bondage and penalty of sin. God's hands are always ready to give us grace so we can receive power to overcome the dysfunction in our lives.

We should depend on God because we need Him to give us the victory over our dysfunctional mindsets that lead to destructive behavior. When we are empowered by God to repent, we are changing our mindset. We are changing our minds so that we may have conduct and conversation that represents and reflects the God that we serve. We are also changing our minds so that we can ultimately have conduct and conversation that does not destroy self and others.

What we have attempted to do and what people have tried get us to do is to be changed from the outside-in. We have addressed our behavior and we have allowed others to addressed our behavior in a way where we did not understand how God works. God's approach and our approach to challenges that we may face are different.

Others have lost patience with us and quite frankly we have lost patience with ourselves. This was due to us not changing at the rate we and others wanted us to change. I have heard Bishop Noel Jones say this in the past, and I am paraphrasing: "The people around us, nor do we set the time-table for our transformation. God does."

What we find out is that God loves us when others do not. We discover that God is patient with us when others are not. God is patient with us when we lose patience with ourselves. God loves us when we do not love ourselves. Others have tried to change us from the outside-in, and we have been attempting to transform ourselves from the outside-in. What we discover is God does not change us from the outside-in; God changes us from the inside-out.

We receive God's Word so that we can change our minds. Changing the mind is where the challenge lies. It is truly a battle. We learn through personal experience that this is something that we cannot do on our own. Changing the mind is something we need God's help to do.

The process of mind renewal is something that will take place for the rest of our lives. Our thinking should always be consistently evolving and being shaped into what God would have it to be. We should not allow the mind to remain stuck in old mindsets.

Whether we are just beginning our walk with God, whether we have been walking with Him for a very long time, or whether we have not begun the journey with God; our thinking has to evolve and revolve around what God would have it to be. There are areas in the mind that need to be renewed. The mind has suffered through childhood issues, pain from previous relationships, and self-inflicted affections.

"The righteous cry out, and the LORD hears, And delivers them out of all their troubles. The LORD is near to those who have a broken heart, And saves such as have a contrite spirit. Many are the afflictions of the righteous, But the LORD delivers him out of them all." (Psalms 34:17-19 NKJV).

Some of our afflictions come from the hands of others. Some of our afflictions are self-inflicted. No matter how we may have been afflicted, the LORD shall deliver us out of them all!

"And do not be conformed to this world, but be transformed by the renewing of your mind, that you may prove what is that good and acceptable and perfect will of God." (Romans 12:2 NKJV). If there is going to be any transformation that takes place in the life of those of us that believe, it will be because the mind is being renewed.

Because we have a desire to please God, we make the mistake of attempting to earn His approval by simply addressing our behavior. What we are learning and discovering is that His approval can never be earned. God's approval is not something that we can work for.

Years of sobriety, months of celibacy or fidelity, or any other righteous behavior cannot wash away our sins. We cannot wash away our sins through good behavior. We also cannot earn God's approval this way either.

The only thing that can wash away our sins is our confidence in the blood of Jesus. The only way we can please God is for us to trust Him or to have faith in Him from the heart. "So then faith comes by hearing, and hearing by the word of God." (Romans 10:17 NKJV). God is pleased when we trust Him.

God is drawing near to us just as we are drawing near to Him. God grants us repentance. Jesus says, "Behold, I stand at the door, and knock. If anyone hears My voice and opens the door, I will come in to him and dine with him, and he with Me." (Revelation 3:20 NKJV).

When we hear the voice or the knock of God on the door of our heart, we want to invite Him. We are making a terrible mistake when we refuse to invite Him in. No matter how difficult it may seem to allow Him into our heart, the last thing we want to do or need to do is to not invite Him in. Despite all the negative things we might have heard about God, we want to push past that and get to know God for ourselves.

Change is difficult. We do not like change because we want to be comfortable. Change is uncomfortable. For us to be transformed by the renewing of our minds, we must learn to be comfortable with being uncomfortable.

Transformation is more than a desire. Transformation is a necessity. We just don't desire God in our lives. We need God in our lives. We have to have Him.

God has brought us to this place in our lives to reveal to us that He is a necessity. Because we see Him as a necessity, we call on Him. My prayer for you and I is that we continue to receive the revelation for the need for God in our lives. My prayer to God for you and I is that we continue to trust Him and to rely upon Him. My prayer to God is that we depend on Him for everything. This is true faith, and when we have this type of faith in God, we truly have a relationship with Him.

The writer of Hebrews says it like this: "But without faith it is impossible to please Him, for he who comes to God must believe that He is, and that He is a rewarder of those who diligently seek Him." (Hebrews 11:6 NKJV).

We do not just believe that God exists. We believe that God is who He says He is. God says He is merciful, so we believe Him. God says He is compassionate, so we believe Him.

God says He is faithful, so we believe Him. God says He is gracious, so we believe Him. We believe that God is, who He says He is, and we seek Him with diligence.

Because we trust God, we have a desire to please Him. We desire to please Him because of the sacrifice that He made. He sacrificed His life for us so that we may live and walk with Him forever. We allow God's Word to strengthen our hearts so that we can change our thinking. We allow God's Word to alter our thinking so that we can grow, mature, develop, and be a blessing in the earth.

Because we are reading this, we are hearing God's voice. Let us continue to allow Him access to our heart. It will be the best decision we will ever make.

To be truthfully honest, the decision has already been made by God because we have been chosen by Him before the world began. We have not chosen Him, but on the contrary, He has chosen us. "According as he hath chosen us in Him before the foundation of the world, that we should be holy and without blame before him in love:" (Ephesians 1:4 KJV).

No man or woman can come to God unless God draws him or her to Him. "No one can come to Me unless the Father who sent Me draws him; and I will raise him up at the last day." (John 6:44 NKJV). God has to draw us, which literally means to drag. He has to drag us because we are either lifeless or putting up resistance. This is the thought process that God wants us to have. God wants us to think as individuals who have been chosen by Him.

"But you are a chosen generation, a royal priesthood, a holy nation, His own special people, that you may proclaim the praises of Him who called you out of darkness into His marvelous light." (1

Peter 2:9 NKJV). We should live our lives with this thought process: we are chosen by God!

We live our lives appreciating Him every day for choosing us. Our God will help us with this. We are not alone. How can we be defeated with this mindset? We cannot because we are persuaded that we belong to Him.

My prayer is that God You help us see that all things are working together for our good; to us that love You and are called according to Your purpose. We appreciate You LORD because You first loved us. Thank you for being for us even when we are not always for ourselves.

My prayer to You God is that You help us to see that we are the head and never the tail. God help us to see that we are above only and never beneath. God help us to see that in spite of our marital status or our financial circumstance that we are more than conquerors through your love. In the name of Jesus, we pray. Amen.

Chapter 2

Loved By Him

It is critical for us to receive God's Word into our hearts so that we can allow Him to change our way of thinking. One of the biggest mistakes that we can make is to believe that God does not love us. When we believe that God does not love us, we do not allow Him to help us to change our perception of Him, our perception of others, and our perception of ourselves.

We want to put our trust in His love for us. We trust that God loves us so that we can allow Him to deal with our negative dispositions and our adverse attitudes. Our adverse attitudes and our negative dispositions cause dysfunctional thinking that lead to destructive behavior.

The belief that God does not love us could come from what we have been taught about God early in our lives. It may stem from the idea that we have to earn God's approval. When we live our lives with this thought process, we either reject God, or we attempt to repair ourselves independent of Him.

"For the LORD does not see as man sees; for man looks at the outward appearance, but the LORD looks at the heart." (I Samuel 16:7b NKJV). We can struggle with the idea that God does not love us when we examine ourselves from an external perspective. We can see ourselves externally, and because we do not like what we see, we can decide not to love ourselves.

Oftentimes the individuals around us see us based on our outward appearance. We are also sometimes viewed based on our egregious and offensive behavior. On these premises people decide not to love us.

Our behavior is a representation or a reflection of what is in our hearts. Our behavior also represents how we think. Behavior is a small representation. It does not tell the entire story.

The belief that God does not love us could come from the very place where we should have been taught that He does. The place that I am referring to is of course church. The House of the LORD is made up of His people. God may be perfect, but we His people are far from that.

I do not condone forsaking the assembly of gathering ourselves together. We should assemble and gather ourselves together in the House of the LORD. I do however understand why people choose not to.

The House of the LORD is supposed to be a hospital. Unfortunately, we God's people sometimes turn it into a courtroom.

So we should assemble. We absolutely should… but I do however understand why and when some people don't.

With all that going on, we also have corruption that exists within leadership in our churches all across this globe. "Then He (Jesus) said to His disciples, 'The harvest truly is plentiful, but the laborers are few.'" (Matthew 9:37 NKJV). One might suggest that this cannot be true because we have churches everywhere. We have bishops, pastors and prophets everywhere. How can the laborers be few?

Well, we see the laborers as being plentiful when we count the corrupt ones. It is hard to find a church that is authentic and it is hard to find a preacher that is genuine. This is why in the preceding verse Jesus says, "Therefore pray the LORD of the harvest to send out laborers into His harvest." (Matthew 9:38 NKJV).

Anytime someone sees us as a commodity, it is because they have a corrupt mind. We are not some man's or some woman's property. We are the property of God. We have been purchased with His own blood. We are the redeemed of the LORD, and we ought to have the boldness, the courage, the audacity and the unmitigated gall to say so. "Let the redeemed of the LORD say so, Whom He has redeemed from the hand of the enemy." (Psalms 107:2 NKJV).

God uses His people to develop us spiritually. Good, bad, or indifferent; it is the people of God that He uses to perfect us. As Bishop Noel Jones put it, "God is the only one that I know that uses imperfect people to perfect people." We should not decide to forsake the assembly of gathering ourselves together because of the wounds that we have received from people who attend, participate, and/or contribute financially to a local assembly.

God has prepared a local assembly for us. When we are wrestling with this, we should ask the LORD to direct our path as it pertains to this issue. We should ask Him to help us to find a church home with fellow believers who believe in the true and living God. Let's also ask the LORD, while He is handing out blessings, to give us a pastor who is after His heart. "And I will give you pastors according to mine heart, which shall feed you with knowledge and understanding." (Jeremiah 3:15 KJV).

When perfection in a church is what we are seeking, we might as well stop seeking. The perfect church does not exist. Most of us have heard this saying before but this is a great time to mention it again. If we were to find the perfect church, and then begin to attend that perfect church, our imperfections would make that perfect church imperfect.

There is no such thing as a perfect church. There is no such thing as a perfect pastor. There is however a such thing as a perfect God. Our perfect God uses imperfect people to perfect us His people.

We are going to ask God to give us the grace to forgive those that have wounded us. People who attend church, participate in church, and/or contribute financially to a local assembly should always love us. This is true. We should always walk in love too and we know that is not always the case.

Since our fellowship with God is a priority, we are going to extend mercy to our brothers and to our sisters in Christ who have wounded us. There is grace for the offenses that we really struggle with getting over. We forgive so that we can heal and receive forgiveness from God for the wounds that we have inflicted on others.

The belief that God does not love us can also be caused by the fact that we may be going through adverse circumstances. It could also be caused by having negative people around us who are reinforcing the condemnatory thoughts that we have towards ourselves. What we have a tendency to do is to give more significance to the opinions of people or to the circumstances that are going on around us. This tendency is causal to the tendency to reduce the significance of what God has spoken in our lives.

Having adverse circumstances is not the biggest opponent to believing that we are loved by God. It is not the negative people around us either. In my humble estimation, the biggest opponent to believing that God loves us is when we have behavior that is negative or directly opposes what God desires for our lives.

God loves us but our enemy the devil is a liar and a deceiver as well. The truth is not in him. The idea that God does not love us is a lie that Satan feeds our minds in order to keep us in a state of perpetual destruction.

We will discuss in-depth in a later chapter our adversary the devil. For the purposes of this discussion, we have an enemy who feeds our minds with lies that are in direct opposition to God's

Word. The purpose of these lies is to keep us from walking with God.

Satan hates us because God loves us. He hates whoever and whatever God loves. Satan's mission is death and destruction.

Jesus, our Savior, says this, "The thief does not come except to steal, and to kill, and to destroy." (John 10:10a NKJV). Satan wants to kill us, steal from us, and he wants to destroy us. That is his mission. But Jesus, our LORD, says, "I have come that they may have life, and that they may have it more abundantly." (John 10:10b NKJV).

When we belief that God loves us, our faith in His love will cause us to move in a positive and constructive direction. Whenever faith or belief is discussed, it pertains to trusting God's Word. Faith in God's Word is more than merely intellectual acceptance or mental assent. It is more than acknowledging that God exists. Faith in God is trusting that He is, Who He says He is.

When God says He is faithful, we believe Him. When God says He is trustworthy, we believe Him. When God says He is merciful, we believe Him. When God says He is gracious, we believe Him.

When God says He is our way-maker, we believe Him. When God say He is our deliverer, we believe Him. When God says, He is our strong tower and our shield, we believe Him.

Faith in God is not intellectual at all. We are always going to have difficulty explaining God to someone who is trying to simply receive Him intellectually. God cannot be received intellectually.

We are going to have a difficult time explaining God to someone who is trying to use logic or human reasoning to try to figure Him out. God cannot be figured out because; "...there is no searching of His understanding." (Isaiah 40:28b KJV).

James says this, "You believe that there is one God. You do well. Even the demons believe...and tremble!" (James 2:19 NKJV). Satan's belief does not produce transformation because he does not depend on God's Word for survival.

An excellent example of intellectual acceptance would be to accept the fact that George Washington was the first president of the United States of America. We were not alive during that time period; but most of us have accepted intellectually what the historians have recorded. With mental assent, we agree with the historians that George Washington was the first president of the United States of America.

The faith that the Bible speaks about, the faith that God's desires for us to have, is for us to put our trust in Him. When we trust God, we rely or depend on His Word for life and survival. When we take God at His Word, we are essentially saying, 'LORD, I need You and LORD I trust You.'

Trusting God is not intellectual at all. Our intellects do not have the capacity to contain someone who is infinite in wisdom, knowledge, and understanding. Trusting God is spiritual. Trusting God is a matter of the heart.

When the adversity we witness though our physical senses tells us that we should be afraid or worried or that we need something destructive to calm our nerves; the Spirit of the Living God speaks to our hearts and says, 'Peace. Be still. I am with you always.'

We believe God with the heart. "For with the heart one believes unto righteousness, and with the mouth confession is made unto salvation." (Romans 10:10 NKJV). We believe with our hearts and therefore we repeat what God has said about us and to us.

Our faith in God produces a positive change because it requires humility, vulnerability, and transparency on our part. We should be transparent enough with God to recognize that the negative behavior in our lives is a direct result of what is in our hearts and also a direct result of how we think. We should be humble enough to see our need for God and to ask him to help us with our destructive ways. We also should be vulnerable enough to trust Jesus the Son of the Living God as our deliver, our way-maker, and as our Savior.

We receive God's love so that we can have the confidence to approach Him in spite of whatever we may be going through. Trusting that God loves us gives us the confidence to approach Him even in spite of our flaws. God loves us in spite of the negative situations that we may be in or in spite of the adverse circumstances that surround our lives.

Sometimes we make the mistake of blaming God or blaming others for circumstances that are created and for situations that we find ourselves in. We should never take responsibility for decisions that other people make. We should only take responsibility decisions that we make. We need God's grace in order to help us to forgive the individual or individuals that have wounded us. We also need God's grace in order to help us to forgive ourselves for when we have wounded ourselves.

We believe that God loves us in spite of the consequences and repercussions that we may be facing; even when those consequences and repercussions are a direct result of our destructive behavior. We believe that God loves us in spite of the hateful people that may be in our lives or the negative people who surround our lives. This refers to people we genuinely care about, and it also refers to the people that we could care less about. Some people we could and should care less about what they have to say and what they may think about us.

Our perception of God and our perception of our circumstances is transformed by His love. God loves us in spite of what we may have done or in spite of what we are doing. It is God's love that encourages us when we are in a negative situation or in a bad relationship.

It is God's love that protects us. It is His love that leads and guides us. It is God's love that lifts us. It is His love that sets us free spiritually and psychologically.

A songwriter wrote, "When nothing else could help, love lifted me." God's choice is to love us because that is who He is. God is love. He loves us in spite of what we may be going through. His love for us is consistent.

Love is more than just an emotion. Love is a decision. Our love for God is not always consistent. Our problem is not that God does not decide to love us.

God always decides to love us. We do not always decide to love Him. Sometimes we do not always decide to love ourselves and other times we do not always decide to love one another.

God is holy. In other words, He is flawless and perfect in all of His ways. He does not make mistakes. We are not a mistake. We may make mistakes, but we are not a mistake.

We need God's love for the mistakes that we make. We need God's grace and His unfailing compassion to work in our lives; so that He can work for us and with us to repair the messes we make.

His love for us was first demonstrated by His work on Calvary's cross. Because we serve a Holy God, He is pure, and there is no unrighteousness in Him. For God to save us, He has to deal with our dysfunction commonly known as sin. God hates dysfunction because when we are not functioning correctly, we are destructive.

God does not deal with our dysfunction from an external vantage point as we would. He does not deal with our sin from an external point of view as the people around us do. He deals with our dysfunction internally.

"The heart is deceitful above all things, and desperately wicked: who can know it?" (Jeremiah 17:9 KJV). God does not simply address our behavior. God goes straight to the source. He deals with our hearts and empowers us to change our minds with His love so that we can live a life that praises and glorifies Him.

God sends His Word coupled with His love for our protection and deliverance. When we do not have a heart and mind to trust God, we open ourselves up for Satan to have his way with us though our evil desires. Because God loves us, He protects us with His Word.

Loved By Him Part II

God always send His Word to bring us life. His Word is just. His Word is good. Our problem is not God's Word; our problem is our carnality and our inability to carry out God's Word without His help.

God who is our benefactor, gives us His Word so that we the recipients of His Word become beneficiaries of His promises. We become beneficiaries of spiritual growth and development. Our spiritual growth and development produces mental health and stability.

Sin causes chaos, confusion, destruction and death. "For God is not the author of confusion but of peace." (I Corinthians 14:33a NKJV). Sin is the author of chaos and confusion. God is the author of wisdom and order. Satan leads us to the believe that God causes confusion. The devil is a liar and the truth is nowhere to be found in him.

When we are completely honest, we cannot recall one time in our lives where sin did not bring with it some heartache and pain. Every-time sin is introduced to us it brings pain, heartache, headache and frustration. We hate sin because we hate what God hates. We hate sin because it destroys our lives and the lives of those around us.

God desires for us to have abundant life. Abundant life is produced by a heart that is filled with the Word of God. It is the Word of God aided by His Spirit in our hearts that gives us the victory over our thoughts and the evil desires that war in our sinful nature.

When God transfers the Word that is in our intellect to our hearts it changes how we think. When we have a mind change, we begin to make decisions that produce life and build life as opposed to making decisions that destroy it. We also through heart repair and mind renewal discover that living for God is more than a desire but an absolute necessity.

Jesus is the King of Glory. The Spirit of the King of Glory is living on the inside of us. "...greater is he that is in you, than he that is in the world." (I John 4:4b KJV) . Because the Great One lives on the inside of us, there is nothing that we cannot overcome.

Salvation in not earned nor is it deserved. Because of the sinful nature that resides in us, we are void of the ability to earn, deserve, or merit eternal life. Salvation is a gift from God that we receive. Receiving this gift produces power to overcome the sinful nature that lies within us. Jesus our Savior set us free from the penalty of sin by the death He died on the cross. "For the wages of sin is death..." (Romans 6:23a KJV).

Jesus our King did not just die, but He rose from the dead. His resurrection gives us dominion over the dysfunction in our lives that has dominated us for far too long. "...but the gift of God is eternal life through Jesus Christ our LORD." (Romans 6:23b KJV).

Christ Jesus is the only one that can put a demand on our lives. He is the only one that loves us with an everlasting love. There is nobody that loves us like Jesus. His love for us is without comparison.

Our spouses cannot love us like Him. Our children cannot love us as He does. Our co-workers, the ones we enjoy working with, and ones we do not enjoy working with, cannot love us like Him. 'Church folks,' the ones we enjoy being around and the ones we would rather avoid cannot love us like Him. The only one that can love us; the way we need to be loved is God through Christ Jesus.

The only one that can demand anything out of our lives is God. Because of the enormous sacrifice He has made He can make demands. Do we know anyone who has made the level of sacrifice for us that God has made? The love that God in Christ demonstrated on Calvary for us qualifies Him to make demands.

God is demanding that we love Him, love self, and love one another. These are His demands and we are the ones that benefit when we do. These are not unreasonable demands. All the ways that God has made for us and all the things that God has brought us out of qualifies Him to demand servant-hood in return to Him.

The beautiful thing about God is that He makes His demands with kindness. The wonderful thing about God is that He makes His demands with gentleness. He implores us and beseeches us; which literally means He begs us because He loves us. God's demands are more like a suggestion. Why choose death, when we have the opportunity to choose life?

God has given us free-will. He has chosen not to over-ride that. God has all-power; and in having all-power He knows how to get us to submit. God does not intimidate us into submission but rather He loves us into submission.

God implores us for our benefit and never for His. He is a God that has absolutely no needs at all. All His needs are met. We are the ones who have the necessities. We need Him. We are not needed by God but we are wanted by Him.

God is qualified to demand because we owe Him a debt that could have only been repaid through eternal death. Being dead in trespasses and dysfunction requires eternal death. "For the wages of sin is death, but the gift of God is eternal life through Jesus Christ our LORD." (Romans 6:23 KJV). God pays our debt for us by sacrificing the life of His Son so that we may have a right to the tree of eternal life.

Jesus our Savior fulfilled God's requirements by obeying every aspect of God's law while He walked the earth. Jesus did what we could not do. His total and complete obedience qualified Him to be the eternal sacrifice for our sin. The penalty for our sins was satisfied through His death, and His death is validated by His own resurrection.

God is not condemning us. God is saving us. God is not judging us. God is rescuing us. Trusting Jesus does not bring judgment. Trusting Jesus brings mercy. We cannot have mercy and judgement. We can only have one or the other. "For judgment is without mercy to the one who has shown no mercy. Mercy triumphs over judgment." (James 2:13 NKJV).

God has put us in position by the death and resurrection of His Son Jesus to decline one so that we can accept the other. We push the decline button on judgment and we hit the accept button on mercy. When judgment calls us, we hit ignore. When mercy calls us, we pick up the phone, and we answer the call and say, 'Hello!!! Where have You been!! I have been looking for You! Thank You!'

The foundation of our faith are these words spoken by Jesus, "For God so loved the world that He gave His only begotten Son, that whoever believes in Him should not perish but have everlasting life." (John 3:16 NKJV). Frequently we stop at this particular verse and overlook the next one. The next verse is critical and just as significant.

Jesus also says this, "For God did not send His Son into the world to condemn the world, but that the world through Him might be saved." (John 3:17 NKJV). This is the bedrock that the Church is built upon. Again, Jesus declares, "…and on this rock, I will build My church, and the gates of Hades shall not prevail against it." (Matthew: 16:18b NKJV).

The rock that we the Church are built upon is the revelation that Jesus is the Christ, the Son of the Living God. He is the Savior of the World. Some of us receive Jesus and unfortunately some of us do not. "But as many as received Him, to them He gave the right to become children of God, to those who believe in His name." (John 1:12 NKJV).

Satan wants us to believe that we are condemned so that he can keep us from coming out from where we are. He is a liar, and the truth is not in him. We are not condemned because Jesus's blood was shed for us. We are not condemned because our King and Savior is not dead but is alive. Goodness and mercy is following us all the days of our life.

We have the mercy of God to get up and to come out of our mess. We have the mercy of God to be free from depression and low self-esteem. We have the mercy of God to walk victoriously. We are not condemned. We are forgiven. We are free. "Therefore if the Son makes you free, you shall be free indeed." (John 8:36 NKJV).

We believe that Jesus was raised from the dead on the third day by the Spirit of God giving Him dominion over all. His resurrection gives us victory over our trespasses and our dysfunction. Without the resurrection, the blood would be powerless. Without the resurrection, our faith would be in a dead sacrifice. The resurrection of Jesus brings power to the blood. His resurrection gives validity and power to the death that He died.

Our trust is not in a dead sacrifice. Our faith is in a sacrifice who rose from the dead with all dominion over all of heaven and earth. Our faith is in Jesus who is alive, who is well, and who is King of Kings and LORD of Lords.

"For the life of the flesh is in the blood, and I have given it to you upon the altar to make atonement for your souls; for it is the blood that makes atonement for the soul." (Leviticus 17:11 NKJV).

The blood that our Savior Jesus shed represents His life being poured out in sacrifice.

The blood that our Savior shed is empowered by His resurrection. Jesus will never experience death again. Therefore, Andrae Crouch, songwriter of the old familiar gospel spiritual, is correct when he accurately composed the song "The Blood Will Never Lose Its Power!"

The Bible says, "(He) Who was delivered up because of our offenses, and raised because of our justification." (Romans 4:25 NKJV). We are justified or declared righteous before God by the death and resurrection of the Son. This was all done before we had any power or ability to love Him in return. Now, if He loves us like this, with His death, while we are in direct opposition to Him, how much more shall He love us by His eternal resurrected life after we belong to Him?

We are truly loved by Him. It is His love that we receive, which in turn causes us to begin to love Him in return, love ourselves, and ultimately love the people around us. Love is a language that is learned. Loving self is unselfishness. God's definition of loving self is sacrificial. When we love God, we will love ourselves.

When we continue to receive God's love we begin to learn what love truly is and how to truly love. Everything we want for ourselves is not always good for us. When we have a desire for something and we then give it to ourselves, that does not mean we are loving ourselves. When someone we care about desires something and we give it to them, that does not mean that we are loving them.

Many times loving self is learning how to tell self no. Sometimes loving others is learning how to tell others no. Some of the things we want for ourselves are not always good for us.

Some of the things we desire are destructive. When loving self and others is compromising or contaminating us, we should question our definition of love. Bishop Noel Jones says this; "we do not love our neighbor more than ourselves but we love our neighbor as ourselves."

It is so paradoxical how loving self and loving others is sacrificial when the stuff that God asks us to sacrifice is destructive to self and others anyway. Is it really a sacrifice if we are giving up something that hurts us and others? The answer is yes. It becomes a sacrifice because of the dependency that we have developed. Unfortunately, that dependency is for someone or something that is only in our lives to make a mess out of our lives.

As we receive God's love, we begin to let go of dysfunctional mindsets and destructive habits. As we mature in love, we begin to hurt ourselves less because the love of God produces self-respect. We love ourselves and respect ourselves because God loves us. I love me because God loves me. "We love him because he first loved us." (I John 4:19 KJV).

We give God the glory for our love for Him because we understand that we could never love Him unless He loves us first.

Our love for God is initiated by Him. Our love for Him would be impossible without His love for us.

Our hearts and our thoughts are controlled by His love. "For the love of Christ controls and compels us." (II Corinthians 5:14a AMP). Loving God correctly and loving self correctly produces the result of loving others correctly.

Our prayer to You Father is that we become convinced that we are loved by You. We pray that You help us to grow spiritually and help us to mature in Your love. Help us to develop character that pleases You.

LORD set us free from dysfunctional thinking that leads to destructive behavior. Father help us to bring You glory so we can be a benefit and an asset to You, to self and to others. Father in the name of Jesus we pray. Amen.

Chapter 3

Grace and Truth

—————————•————————

When God speaks, or when God sends His Word to us, He sends His Word with the intent and with the purpose to bring us closer to Him. God desires a relationship with us. His Word is designed to get into our hearts so that we can use His Word to change how we think. God desires for us to be transformed out of the world and into what He would have us to be.

Transformation is a process. We live in the world, but we are being transformed out of the world by His Word. Bishop Noel Jones said it like this, "We are being transformed from being world thinkers to being Word thinkers."

God first captures the heart with His love with the purpose of giving us the opportunity to change our minds; so that our behavior ultimately reflects who He is. Without His Word we would never believe Him. "So then faith comes by hearing, and hearing by the word of God." (Romans 10:17 NKJV). Truth is the foundation to our relationship with God. Our relationship with Him is founded on

His Word. Christ Jesus is our foundation. "For no other foundation can anyone lay than that which is laid, which is Jesus Christ." (I Corinthians 3:11 NKJV).

Our relationship with God is founded upon grace and truth which is in Christ Jesus. "For the law was given through Moses, but grace and truth came through Jesus Christ." (John 1:17 NKJV). Grace is also part of the foundation that allows us to enter into the Kingdom of God. Grace is what takes us from being God's enemy to now being His child. Grace brings us from darkness to light. Grace is also necessary for us to maintain a relationship with God.

Grace is necessary because we never get to a place where we arrive in God. We never get to a place where we do not need Him. No matter the victories we have had in our walk with God, we still need God's grace. Whether it is overcoming alcohol or drug addiction, overcoming illicit sexual behavior, overcoming an eating disorder, or a particular attitude or disposition, we never get to a place where we do not need God's grace.

For us to maintain a relationship with God, we have to fight just to remain humble. This is the battle that is going on in our minds. It is the battle of pride vs. humility. The devil wants us high-minded or in other words arrogant. Arrogance keeps us at a place where we are unable to see self in proper light.

When we have an incorrect perception of self, we are led down a path of destruction. God desires for us to remain humble so that we can receive all that He has for us to receive. The difference between being proud and being humble is that when we are proud, we need God, we just don't know it. When we are humble, we not only need Him, but we know that we do.

The challenge is not just comparing self to others. The challenge is oftentimes comparing self to self. The challenge is sometimes taking self and comparing self to how dysfunctional self use to be to the growth that has taken place.

We should celebrate what we have overcome because we want to always continue to appreciate what the LORD has done for us. There is an appropriate time for celebration. We do however have to win the battle in our minds that wants us to continue to celebrate our victories. There are times when we can celebrate our victories too long. Allow me to explain.

We want to celebrate what and where God has brought us from. We do not want to celebrate our victories to the place where we never press forward to win the other battles that we must face in our lives. God desires for us to always to continue to grow. It is true that for us to continue to grow, we must to put our failures behind us. We must also put our successes behind us as well.

For us to drive our lives successfully we do not drive our lives staring though the rear-view mirror. To drive our lives successfully we stare though the windshield. We use the rear-view mirror on occasion to make necessary adjustments.

Our experiences are our precedent with God to overcome the challenges we face today and the challenges we have to face tomorrow. We never want to discard our testimony. Whenever we are going through something we use our experiences or our testimony to remind us that if God brought us out the last time then He will bring us out again.

We have our testimony in proper perspective when it is in agreement with how gracious and merciful God has been to us. We are then equipped to overcome whatever Satan might throw our way. "And they overcame him by the blood of the Lamb and by the word of their testimony." (Revelation 12:11a NKJV).

A good analogy to use is this one. Michael Jordan is regarded by many as the greatest basketball player who ever lived. Michael Jordan won 6 NBA championships during his NBA career. This man with help from teammates, coaches, front-office and training staff of course, won 3 championships in a row, twice.

Michael Jordan and the Chicago Bulls accomplished an amazing feat by 'three-peating' twice. It would have been challenging to win the second championship continuing to celebrate the first one. Or win the second one continued to celebrate the third one; and so forth and so on.

We celebrate our victories for the appropriate time, and then we use our experiences to overcome the next challenge. We have to face the battle, win the battle, and celebrate the victory. We then move on to the next challenge in our lives being reminded of what God has done for us in the past. We have to be reminded because the next challenge will be greater than the last. We do not faint because if God did it for us and through us before, He will do it for us and through us again.

We do this with a heart that is being repaired and with a mind that is being reconstructed by God's Word. "Brethren, I count not myself to have apprehended: but this one thing I do, forgetting those things which are behind, and reaching forth unto those things which are before, I press toward the mark for the prize of the high calling of God in Christ Jesus." (Philippians 3:13-14 KJV).

We also make a mistake when we compare ourselves to others. When we compare ourselves to someone other than Jesus Christ, we become either high-minded or low-minded depending on how we feel about ourselves and the person(s) we are comparing ourselves to. When we think more lowly of ourselves than we ought to, we began to develop an inferiority complex. We get into the spirit of heaviness or depression in chapter twelve of this book so stay tuned.

When we think more highly of ourselves than we ought to, we began to develop a superiority complex. This mentality or mindset is the embodiment of pride. Pride is something we want and need to avoid at all costs because it removes us from the presence of God.

Pride is disrespect to God. When we are arrogant, we are showing God disrespect. Pride will blind us and it will also cause us to mishandle people. To stay free from pride, there is no question in my mind that this is something that we need God's help to do. "But He gives more grace. Therefore, He says: God resists the proud, But gives grace to the humble." (James 4:6 NKJV).

"Pride goes before destruction, And a haughty spirit before a fall." (Proverbs 16:18 NKJV). For us to receive God's grace, God frequently has to humble us through correction or commonly referred to as chastening in the King James Version of the Bible. Our negative experiences force us to humble ourselves before Him. We receive revelation about ourselves when we go through something.

David says this in the 23rd Psalms, "Your rod and Your staff, they comfort me." (Psalms 23:4b NKJV). The question that comes to mind is: How does His rod comfort us when His rod causes pain? His staff is for guidance so we understand how God leading us and guiding us can be comforting; but how does something that brings us pain give us comfort?

We are comforted by His rod also because God only corrects or chastens His children. We are comforted by His rod because it is evidence that we belong to Him. God does not correct illegitimate children. The mere fact that He corrects us comforts us because if He did not correct us, it would signify that we were not His. "For whom the LORD loves He chastens, And scourges every son whom He receives." (Hebrews 12:6 NKJV). When we receive correction, God deals with us as children.

Correction may be painful. It may even be grievous because God is literally performing surgery. Physical surgery can be painful and so is spiritual surgery.

God is making corrections. God is repairing our heart and correcting our mindset. We just have to hold on to the exhortation that says, "For His anger is but for a moment, His favor is for life; Weeping may endure for a night, But joy comes in the morning." (Psalms 30:5 NKJV).

Correction may be painful but it is for our benefit. "Now no chastening seems to be joyful for the present, but painful; nevertheless, afterward it yields the peaceable fruit of righteousness to those who have been trained by it." (Hebrews 12:11 NKJV). We appreciate God for loving us enough to repair us and to correct us.

It is critical that as soon as God reveals to us that pride is in our heart and that pride is in our thinking that we acknowledge it. What we must do is agree with Him about it. We should not disagree with God about it but we should agree with Him.

Our confession is, 'LORD, You are right and I am wrong. My heart and my thinking are consumed with pride and I humble myself before You. I need your mercy and your grace.' We are going to acknowledge our dysfunction and come into agreement with God about our sin; so that He can release us from it. This is necessary so that we may have proper perspective of life and proper perception as it pertains to the people around us.

God wants us to understand that when we approach Him, that we are not approaching a throne of judgment. On the contrary we are approaching a throne of grace. Since we are approaching a throne of grace, this gives us an opportunity to be transparent with God. If we were approaching a throne of judgment, then we would have a reason to be fearful when we approach Him. Since we are approaching a throne of grace, then we approach Him with boldness.

Because we are approaching a throne of grace, we have access to God even while we are dysfunctional in our thinking and destructive in our behavior. It is not our sin that keeps us from Him.

It's our pride. God does not resist the sinner. He resists the proud. God will receive us as sinners when we as sinners humble ourselves and ask Him for mercy.

Because God is so gracious and so compassionate, we approach Him with boldness, ask for forgiveness, and receive the grace that we need to overcome our struggle. "Let us, therefore, come boldly to the throne of grace, that we may obtain mercy and find grace to help in time of need." (Hebrews 4:16 NKJV).

David says this, "Keep back Your servant also from presumptuous sins; Let them not have dominion over me. Then I shall be blameless, And I shall be innocent of great transgression." (Psalms 19:13 NKJV). Presumptuous is defined as (of a person or their behavior) failing to observe the limits of what is permitted or appropriate. In the verse that precedes this one, David says, "Who can understand his errors? Cleanse me from secret faults." (Psalms 19:12 NKJV).

Sometimes as we go through life, we think we understand ourselves, but oftentimes, we really do not understand ourselves like we think we do. Often we think we really have it all together; but most times we do not have it all together like we think we do.

There are times when sin is not evident because of a lack of opportunity. We are not always as strong as we think we are. This is why we should not be condemnatory toward others when they are struggling. We should pray as David prayed because there could be a secret fault in us that just has not had the opportunity to manifest itself.

Our prayer to God is that He keep us from presumptuous sins so that they do not dominate us though how we speak to one another and how we speak to ourselves. "Let the words of my mouth and the meditation of my heart Be acceptable in Your sight, O LORD, my strength and my Redeemer." (Psalms 19:14 NKJV). Our humility will usher in the grace of God into our lives.

For years we saw the grace of God as liberty to sin. Now as we are maturing in God, we see God's grace as our way out of sin. His grace is what gives us the ability to deny ourselves and to put the devil under our feet.

Humility allows us also to be compassionate towards others. When we are moving and living with compassion towards others, we know that we are getting closer to God and becoming more like Him. God is full of compassion.

If God were not compassionate, we would not be here right now. We do not even want to imagine where we would be without His compassion. We do not want to imagine where we would be without His goodness and His mercy.

We deserve judgment. We deserve eternal damnation; but God had, and has, and will continue to have His hand of compassion on us. All we have to do is receive it.

The definition of grace is un-merited, un-earned, un-deserved favor. We do not earn God's favor; we receive it. "For by grace you have been saved through faith, and that not of yourselves; it is the gift of God, not of works, lest anyone should boast." (Ephesians 2:8-9 NKJV).

Because we have carnal minds that are in the process of being renewed, we sometimes become high-minded and self-righteous in our thinking. We think we were the ones who brought ourselves out of our mess. No sir. No ma'am. "Through the LORD's mercies we are not consumed, because His compassions fail not. They are new every morning; Great is Your faithfulness." (Lamentations 3:22-23 NKJV).

It is the goodness of the LORD that keeps us from utterly destroying ourselves. God is patient and He is kind. God is gentle and He is empathetic. He has been so good to us. This is not just something that we have read; this is something that we are experiencing. His grace saves us and empowers us to maintain a relationship with Him.

My prayer for us is that You LORD continue to enlighten us and reveal Yourself to us as we journey through this thing called life. LORD show us those errors in our lives that are not totally and completely surrendered to You. My prayer to You LORD is that we continue to approach your throne of grace, that we may receive your mercy and receive your grace to help in the time of need. Amen.

Chapter 4

We Walk By Faith

———————————
·●·

"Now in the fourth watch of the night, Jesus went to them, walking on the sea. And when the disciples saw him walking on the sea, they were troubled, saying, 'It is a ghost!' And they cried out for fear. But immediately Jesus spoke to them, saying, 'Be of good cheer! It is I; do not be afraid.' And Peter answered Him and said, 'LORD, if it is You, command me to come to You on the water.' So He said, 'Come.' And when Peter had come down out of the boat, he walked on the water to go to Jesus. But when he saw the wind was boisterous, he was afraid; and beginning to sink, he cried, saying, 'LORD, save me!' And immediately Jesus stretched out His hand and caught him, and said to him, 'O you of little faith, why did you doubt?' And when they were come into the boat, the wind ceased. Then those who were in the boat came and worshiped Him, saying, 'Truly You are the Son of God.'" (Matthew 14:25-33 NKJV).

This is a very familiar passage of Scripture and an accurate depiction of our walk with God. When we look at this passage of

Scripture, we see Jesus doing something miraculous by walking on water. We also see Peter desiring to do the miraculous by going after the LORD.

This is where God wants us. He wants us to come after Him even if it seems impossible to reach Him. God wants us to defy the odds and have dominion over the situation and go after Him. God can always be reached. We just have to receive His invitation.

Peter says, "LORD, if it is You, command me to come to You on the water." (Matthew14:28 NKJV). Jesus gives the invitation and says, "Come." God's invitation is His Word. Jesus invites Peter to come, and He begins to do what is impossible without God and walks on water.

Physics says Peter should sink. God's Word says, "If you can believe, all things are possible to him who believes." (Mark 9:23 NKJV). When God invites us, then we can by faith in God defy the odds and do the impossible. "With men this is impossible, but with God all things are possible." (Matthew 19:26b NKJV).

Peter's circumstances begin to become adverse. He takes his mind off the Master and places his mind on the storm that is going on around him. When our minds are on our situation, we begin to sink into hopelessness. When our minds are on our adversity, we begin to drown in despair. The beautiful thing about Jesus is that even when we begin to drown into hopelessness and we begin to sink into despair; when we holla' out to the LORD for help, He will rescue us and not allow us to drown.

Then Jesus says to Peter, "O you of little faith, why did you doubt?" (Matthew14:31b NKJV). This question is designed to bring self-reflection. Self-reflection takes us into prayer.

'Heavenly Father, why do we doubt when LORD, You are with us? Why do we doubt when LORD, You are greater than our storm? Why do we doubt when LORD, You are greater than our circumstances and our situation? We doubt You and begin to sink when we focus on the adversity. We do not need to doubt. We can do the impossible and overcome the circumstance and the situation when we keep our mind focused on You.'

When we study Scripture, we want to study it with an open mind and with an open heart. It is important when studying God's Word to be as objective as possible. We do not want to be subjective in thought at all.

When we are subjective in thought, we are searching the Scriptures to prove that our ideas and/or concepts are correct. When we are objective in thought, we are open to receive what God has to say to us.

Jesus says this, "You search the Scriptures, for in them you think you have eternal life; and these are they which testify of Me." (John 5:39 NKJV). Jesus is the centrifugal force of all Scripture. The definition of centrifugal force is an apparent force that acts outward on a body moving around a center, arising from the body's inertia.

Jesus is the center of all Scripture. Jesus is the apparent force acting outward towards us His body, as we move around Him whom is our center. The correct interpretation of Scripture always brings us closer to Jesus.

We need God to reveal Himself to us. For God to reveal Himself to us, His Word has to become personal. We cannot speak for anyone else but ourselves when we need revelation from Him. We can only speak for ourselves.

Each and every time we study or read His Word, we want and need to be as open-minded as humanly possible. What we want to do is pray, 'LORD, open up my heart so I can receive your Word. Let your Word get into my heart so that I can use it to renew my mind.'

When we are closed-minded, we read the Word with a lot of ideas. We have a tendency to attempt to make God's Word prove concepts that we have built up in our thinking. These concepts come from previous experiences or just simply incorrect teaching or preaching of Scripture.

God's Word is true, absolute, and always consistent. When we attempt to alter His Word in any way we make His Word ineffective in our lives and in the lives of others. Everything else around us may change. Circumstances fluctuate and situations change; people come and go but God's Word remains the same. "Jesus Christ is the same yesterday, today, and forever." (Hebrews 13:8 NKJV).

"Looking unto Jesus the author and finisher of our faith..." (Hebrews 12:2a NKJV). Jesus is the composer and the publisher of our faith walk. We make mistakes in presenting God's Word if our presentation is founded upon our own ideas and concepts. We can also make mistakes in our presentation when we use a condemnatory attitude and a condensing disposition.

We should always use compassion when presenting Jesus to others. We should make suggestions and recommendations and not demands. Jesus has to be received. Some of us receive Him and unfortunately some of us do not.

Jesus is a gift that we receive. We persuade or we convince that Jesus is a necessity. We do however do this with the understanding that we can only give others Jesus when they decide to take Him for themselves.

God wants us patience. God wants us kind. God wants us meek and gentle. God did not give us the Holy Spirit to control other people. God gave us the Holy Spirit so that we could control ourselves.

His Word is the foundation of our faith walk. When we read God's Word, we read it ready to receive from God so that His Word can speak directly to us. His Word comes to repair our hearts and to help us to renew our minds. His Word comes to give us the opportunity to change how we think.

"Wisdom is the principal thing; Therefore get wisdom. And in all your getting, get understanding." (Proverbs 4:7 NKJV). The beginning of understanding is wisdom. The beginning of wisdom is knowledge. The beginning of knowledge is the fear of God. "The fear of the LORD is the beginning of knowledge, But fools despise wisdom and instruction." (Proverbs 1:7 NKJV).

When we fear God, we respect Him or revere Him. We are not afraid of God we respect Him. We are not in terror of God; we hold Him in high esteem or in high regard. Our respect for God is where knowledge begins.

Any knowledge that we have is vain; when at the beginning of our knowledge we do not hold God in high regard. We should revere God. We should respect Him.

Knowledge in its most simplistic definition is information. The knowledge of God is simple, but to have the knowledge of God, we must respect Him. God is to be revered. "Then you will understand the fear of the LORD, And find the knowledge of God." (Proverbs 2:5 NKJV).

The knowledge of God is very important because, the knowledge of God provides protection. The knowledge of God works as a hedge of protection against making foolish choices and undisciplined decisions. The Bible declares, "My people are destroyed for lack of knowledge. Because you have rejected knowledge, I also will reject you, from being priest for Me; Because you have forgotten the law of your God, I will also forget your children. The more they increased, The more they sinned against Me; I will change their glory into shame." (Hosea 4:6,7 NKJV).

When we pay close attention to this particular passage of Scripture, we find that it is not the lack of knowledge that is leading to our demise. Knowledge is always available The knowledge of God is all around us. What is bringing our demise is our rejection of knowledge. We have refused to apply the information that God gives us to our lives. God works in the application of knowledge.

Here is wisdom. Wisdom is when we are not hearers of the Word only but doers also. Wisdom is when we have the heart and the mind to take what we know about God and apply it to our lives.

A great example of this is that in America red stop signs are used to notify us that while we are driving and approaching an intersection we are to stop at that intersection. Knowledge is when we know to stop when we see a red stop sign. Wisdom is when we take that knowledge and apply it while we are driving. When we are foolish, we run through the intersection without stopping first. When we are wise, we stop. Wisdom is when we actually stop.

God does not want us to just hear His Word. God desires that we do His Word. He desires that we be wise. We are ignorant when we do not know. We are foolish when we do not do what we know to do. My prayer for you and I is that God strengthen us to not only increase in knowledge but to increase in wisdom. My prayer for you and I is that we be not hearers only but doers also. 'LORD help us to renew our minds so that we may be wise in these last and evil days.'

We read or study God's Word not to just increase in knowledge or to simply to accumulate information. We read and study God's Word so that it can get into our hearts and we use it to change how we think so that His Word can be applied to our lives. We are in need of a mind change.

It would be foolish on our part to just simply increase in information, teach others and never apply it to our own lives. We should save self-first before we try to save others. "Be saved from this perverse generation." (Acts 2:40b NKJV). We allow God's Word to be deposited into our hearts so that we can change our minds and be transformed into who God would have us to be. The process of mind renewal will qualify or equip us to handle people.

Side note: Mind renewal is not an event that transpires in our lives. Mind renewal is a process of transformation that will continue for the rest of our lives. "Therefore, we do not lose heart. Even though our outward man is perishing, yet the inward man is being renewed day by day." (II Corinthians 4:16 NKJV).

Wisdom is the most important thing in our lives. It is the most significant thing. It is first in order or first in importance. We must get wisdom. Wisdom is when we take information and apply it to self.

Prayer is an important component to wisdom as well. "If any of you lacks wisdom, let him ask of God, who gives to all liberally, and without reproach, and it will be given to him." (James 1:5 NKJV). When we receive the revelation that we lack wisdom our first response should be to ask God for help.

"And in all your getting, get understanding." (Proverbs 4:7b NKJV). Understanding is simply compassion or empathy for others.

As we revisit the scenario with the stop sign, we have an understanding when we have the compassion that is required to teach others how to stop when they see a red stop sign. Understanding is vital when helping others because having an understanding eradicates having a condemnatory attitude and a condescending disposition. Having an understanding eliminates arrogance in the leader or in the teacher.

We cannot help people when we think we are superior to others and others are inferior to us; when others have a problem that we do not have. We cannot help people when we think we are superior to others and others are inferior to us; when others have a problem that we use to have. We cannot help people when we think we are superior to others and others are inferior to us; when others have a problem that we have never had.

For us to be effective in helping people, we have to feel what they are feeling. Feeling what someone is feeling is empathy or compassion. Having empathy or compassion for someone means to have an understanding.

Arrogance is a monster. Pride is very easy to detect in others but very difficult to detect in self. This is why self-awareness is so critical to our spiritual growth and development. When we operate with a superiority complex, it is psychologically debilitating to the people we are assigned to help because it discourages and depletes energy. No doubt wisdom is principle because we want and need to gather information and apply it to self; but with everything we gather let us gather an understanding so we can be a blessing to somebody else.

When we have an understanding, we have the patience to teach others to stop. When we have an understanding, we have the compassion to help others stop. When we have an understanding, we have empathy for others because our experiences remind us that there was a time in our lives when we struggled with stopping at that red stop sign.

God wants to take us from feeling sorry for one another to feeling what each other is feeling. When we have compassion or understanding, we feel what one another is feeling while they are going through. Jesus feels what we are feeling. "For we do not have a High Priest who cannot sympathize with our weaknesses, but was in all points tempted as we are, yet without sin." (Hebrews 4:15 NKJV).

God feels what we are feeling. He does not feel sorry for us sorry for us because, "as His divine power has given to us all things that pertain to life and godliness, through the knowledge of Him who called us by glory and virtue." (II Peter 1:3 NKJV). God will not enable us by feeling sorry for us but on the contrary, He empowers us because He feels what we feel.

When we are going through something difficult, God is able to assist us in times of hardship and great distress. "For in that He Himself has suffered, being tempted, He is able to aid those who are tempted." (Hebrews 2:18 NKJV). Jesus feels our pain.

Mind renewal is very challenging to say the least. There is no way we can allow God to take us through the process of mind renewal and not have compassion for those who are wrestling with something in their minds. As we grow in understanding, we become empathetic to those that are battling in the same process.

Dealing with self and seeing self in proper light allows us to see others in the proper light. Changing how we think is a battle. There is not a day that goes by that we do not need God to help us to renew our minds. Mind renewal is truly a process that occurs day by day. We should gain an understanding before we attempt to lead and teach other people.

"And why do you look at the speck in your brother's eye, but do not consider the plank in your own eye? Or how can you say to your brother, 'Let me remove the speck from your eye'; and look, a plank is in your own eye? Hypocrite! First remove the plank from your own eye, and then you will see clearly to remove the speck from your brother's eye." (Matthew 7:3-5 NKJV).

What Jesus is teaching us here is that a lack a self-awareness causes blindness. The inability to deal with self-births an attitude that is condescending, judgmental, and high-minded. This negative disposition will have an adverse impact on self and others. When we have a telephone pole hanging out of our eye, we injure self and others with this telephone pole. We must first remove it before attempting to remove specks from other people's eyes.

When we see self and others properly we see ourselves as having the telephone pole and others as having the specks. We should not get this twisted. It is not the other way around. To be effective we must all learn and embrace this principle: "This is a faithful saying and worthy of all acceptance, that Christ Jesus came into the world to save sinners, of whom I am chief." (I Timothy 1:15 NKJV).

"Blessed is the man Who walks not in the counsel of the ungodly, Nor stands in the path of sinners, Nor sits in the seat of the scornful; But his delight is in the law of the LORD, And in His law he meditates day and night. He shall be like a tree Planted by the rivers of water, That brings forth its fruit in its season, Whose leaf also shall not wither; And whatever he does shall prosper." (Psalms 1:1-3 NKJV).

God blesses us when we decide that His counsel is better than ungodly counsel. Let us make the Word of God our delight. We can receive ungodly counsel from ungodly people. Truth be told, we can receive ungodly counsel from godly people. We should learn to use discernment over our loyalty to a particular person or to a particular organization when receiving advise.

When we use loyalty, we receive every word. When we use discernment, we decide which words to receive. "Beloved, do not believe every spirit, but test the spirits, whether they are of God; because many false prophets have gone out into the world." (I John 4:1 NKJV).

God says we will be like trees planted by rivers of water, that brings forth fruit in our season. He says our leaf shall not wither.

Also, whatever we put our hands to shall prosper. The Word of God directs our path.

Our relationship with God reveals what our gifts and what our talents are. God reveals what He has placed us on this earth to do. That way we are not going after someone else's dream or what someone else would have for us to do. We go after God who fulfills our dreams and blesses whatever it is He wants to put our hands to do. God says whatever we do will prosper or be successful.

'LORD we pray that You give us something to do so we can be prosperous.' We want to be successful. The devil is a lie. We want to be the giver rather be the one needing a gift. 'LORD we pray that You cause us to prosper so we can bring You glory, be a blessing to self, and be a blessing to others.'

God is patient towards us. God is compassionate toward us. This is the God that we experience. We experience His love. This is the God that we teach and preach.

My prayer for you and I is that God increase the knowledge of Him so that we may become wiser. 'Also LORD as you give us wisdom, give us understanding so that we can be a blessing to one another. Help us to walk by faith and not by sight. In Jesus name we pray, Amen.

Chapter 5

There Will Be Peace

———————
•

One of the things that I have struggled with in my life is anxiety. When others or completely honest they will tell you that they have struggled with this as well. Anxiety is defined by the Mayo Clinic as intense, excessive, and persistent worry and fear about everyday situations. We need to break down the words, intense, excessive, and persistent before we move on.

Intense is defined as extreme force, degree, or strength. Excessive is defined as more than is necessary, normal, or desirable. Persistent is defined as continuing to exist or endure over a prolonged period.

When we are wrestling with anxiety, our struggle is with something that is of extreme force, something that is more than necessary or normal, and continues to exist over a prolonged period of time. It is fear over everyday situations and circumstances. Worry is very powerful and very real. It can be caused by having financial hardship, the loss of a loved one through death or divorce, or over the threat of sickness or disease. It can lead to discouragement, frustration, depression, alcohol and or drug dependency and it can also ultimately lead to suicide and/or homicide.

Anxiety can also be caused by making a mistake. We can 'beat ourselves up' over what we did or what we did not do. We can play the 'shoulda,' 'coulda,' 'woulda' game with our minds too long and that can also lead to stress and anxiety.

Anxiety occurs when our thoughts are fixated on a situation that we really do not want to be in and/or on adverse circumstances going on around us. Oftentimes what is occurring is not what we want for our lives. We want this situation to change. We want God to move and fix this. We want God to alter the situation but He has not changed it. Our frustration grows and disappointment occurs because God is not doing what we want Him to do.

Now we are already anxious. We are already fearful over a particular circumstance or situation and when we call on God, He does not change what we want Him to change. In our minds we are fearful that this situation is going to lead to our demise or that the situation is going to lead to our destruction.

What we do to prevent the doom and destruction is panic. Whenever we panic we make irrational decisions. When we panic, we make bad choices not governed by God's will for our lives. Instead of trusting God, we use our fear to take matters into our own hands.

Anxiety rests in our hearts and it puts an extreme amount of pressure on the mind. Our situations are very real and our circumstances are real. The fear that we are not going to survive however is not.

As we mature in God, we discover that anxiety is a decision. We are learning that fear is a choice. We are stronger than we oftentimes think. Worry has to be a decision or God would not say through Paul, "Be anxious for nothing, but in everything by prayer and supplication with thanksgiving, let your requests be made known to God. And the peace of God, which surpasses all comprehension, will guard your hearts and your minds in Christ Jesus." (Philippians 4:6-7 NASB).

Thoughts filled with fear are governed by satanic forces and are designed to keep us from moving closer to the LORD. What we discover is that God is able to use negative situations and adverse circumstances when we trust Him. God will use our problems including the people we really do not want to be around to develop our character when we acknowledge Him.

The Scripture declares to "Trust in the LORD with all your heart, And lean not on your own understanding; In all your ways acknowledge Him, And He shall direct your paths." (Proverbs 3:5-6 NKJV).

We acknowledge the situation and we should. We acknowledge the circumstance and we should. We should also acknowledge that God is bigger than our situation. We should also acknowledge that God is bigger than our circumstance.

What God wants to do is feed our spirits with His Word so that our thoughts can be detached from what we are going through. God desires that we develop a mind that is focused squarely on Him. When we have a mind that is focused on Him, we will take direction from our God and not take directions from our circumstances and/or situations.

We need a Word from the LORD. We need God to speak to our spirits through His Word so that our thoughts can be released from our situation and/or circumstances. We need a Word from the LORD so that we can be set free from complaining and delivered into praising Him.

We will discuss this more in the next chapter but complaining weakens us. It not only weakens us when we complain but it also weakens the feeble-minded people around us. We overcome complaining with our praise for God.

We praise God and tell God how good He is not because He is insecure. God is very secure in who He is. God knows who He is. We do not praise God because He does not know who He is. We praise God because we are the ones that need to know who He is.

Satan wants us complaining so He can steal our strength. We praise God because praise ushers in joy; "for the joy of the LORD is your strength." (Nehemiah 8:10b NKJV). We need strength for our circumstances and our situations. We need strength for our relationships and for our lives.

We fight to eradicate complaining and to incorporate praising. Whenever we complain we are hurting ourselves. Let us from this day forward do our best to decree and declare that, "I will bless the LORD at all times; His praise shall continually be in my mouth." (Psalms 34:1 NKJV).

The Word of God that is in our hearts will change our perspective. What God wants us to see and what we need to see is that He is in complete control even when our situation is out of control. No matter what situation we are allowing to cause us anxiety, the answer is in our God. Our perspective of Him determines how we approach Him.

As discussed in the last chapter, there is a significant difference between knowledge and wisdom. There is a difference between what we know intellectually and what is in our hearts. There is a difference between what is in our head and what is in our spirits. How we handle adversity reveals to us when His Word is hidden in our memory or hidden in our heart.

Our God who sits high and looks low does not need our permission to try our faith. He will allow us to go through a series of trials that will reveal our character. When we allow God's Word to keep our heart free from offense, we will see that all things are working together for our good. God who loves us dearly is using our adversity to bring us closer to Him. Our trials force us to trust Him.

"But in everything by prayer and supplication with thanksgiving let your requests be made known to God." (Philippians 4:6b NASB). When we pray, we want to pray with thanksgiving or with appreciation for God. Paul also says, "For I have learned in whatever state I am, to be content." (Philippians 4:11 NKJV).

Contentment is a word that is too often avoided because we think it suggest a negative connotation. When God says we should be content, it sounds like He is saying be lethargic, be apathetic or lack ambition. This could not be any further from the truth.

Contentment does not mean that we are not allowed to desire better. Contentment does not mean that we are not allowed to strive for better or that we are to be absent of ambition. The devil is a lie. That's not the psychology that God wants us to have. Contentment suggests peace. It suggests tranquility.

God is not saying be content with the negative situation. He is saying be content in the negative situation. God is not saying be content with the adverse circumstance. He is saying be content in the adverse circumstance. God is not saying be content with the bad relationship. He is saying be content in the bad relationship. God is saying be content or be at peace because I will never leave you nor forsake you. When we have peace that surpasses all understanding, we make better decisions.

"Let your conduct be without covetousness; be content with such things as you have. For He Himself has said, 'I will never leave you nor forsake you.' So we may boldly say: 'The LORD is my helper; I will not fear. What can man do to me?'" (Hebrews 13:5-6 NKJV).

The LORD is with us. "God is our refuge and strength; a very present help in trouble." (Psalms 46:1 KJV). When our minds are on our situation, we have anxiety. When our minds are in a state of worship for our God and appreciation for Him, we have peace that surpasses all understanding.

God does not want for us to grow bitter and run from Him. When we do that we are making a terrible mistake. "Pursue peace with all people, and holiness, without which no one will see the LORD: looking carefully lest anyone fall short of the grace of God; lest any root of bitterness springing up cause trouble, and by this many become defiled;" (Hebrews 12:15 NKJV).

Bitterness will cause us to stop seeking God's grace. We need God's grace. His grace is the last thing we need to be running from. We need His grace to make it through our trials. Unfortunately, tribulation is a part of all of our lives. This is not something that we can avoid.

When we have adversity, the question now becomes; Are we going back to drugs and alcohol, or are we running to the LORD? Are we going back to that relationship that we begged God to set us free from, or are we turning to the LORD? Are we going to take our lives and/or take someone else life, or are we turning to the LORD?

The devil is a lie and the truth is not in him. We are emphatically turning to the LORD! We are going to feed our hearts the Word of God and call on the name of the LORD so that we receive strength to do what we know we should do.

What we are facing can be so intense that we feel like we are losing our minds because of what we are going through. What the Word of God does is arrest our hearts and empowers us to change our thoughts so that we can now begin to see the LORD who is reigning over our circumstances and our situation. God wants us to begin to see Him who is not just reigning over us but He who is in us and with us while we are going through.

As children of God, we are citizens of God's Kingdom. God's government is not a democracy. His government is a kingdom. We are members of the Kingdom of God.

We do not participate in writing God's law. God writes the laws and for us to have divine wisdom, we walk within the perimeters that He has set. God does not serve us, we serve Him.

"'You are My witnesses', says the LORD, 'And My servant whom I have chosen, That you may know and believe Me, And understand that I am He. Before Me there was no God formed, Nor shall there be after Me. I, even I, am the LORD, And besides Me there is no savior.'" (Isaiah 43:10-11 NKJV).

"I am the LORD, and there is no other; There is no God besides Me. I will gird you, though you have not known Me, that they may know from the rising of the sun to its setting That there is none besides Me. I am the LORD, and there is no other." (Isaiah 45:5-6 NKJV).

Do we need God to change our situation before we can give Him praise? Do we need God to change our circumstances before we can worship Him? Do we need God to bring us out before we give Him glory? Absolutely not! We move and better our lives with the peace of God, and we receive the peace of God when we praise Him and worship Him for who He is.

Before we receive the Spirit of God, He is with us. As believers God is with us. After we receive the Spirit of God He is in us. We grow in the knowledge of God because without spiritual development our character will resemble that of an unbeliever.

At the beginning of our walk with God, we do not understand the significance of human responsibility. We think God does everything for us. As we begin to grow in the knowledge of God, we learn that He works with us and through us.

God does a lot for us. Absolutely, no question; but much of what God does in our lives is what He does in us and through us. We have a partnership with God. He is the senior partner and we are the junior partner.

Trusting God puts us in a hard place because trusting Him makes us vulnerable. Trusting Him is the only way we can please Him. In order for us to trust God, we have to believe that He will reward us when we seek Him.

We know the LORD is coming back to get us. We are looking forward to His return. It is also good to expect to see the goodness of the LORD in the land of the living. Both statements are true. One statement does not exclude the other.

We will faint or 'throw in the towel' when we do not live our lives with expectation. David said, "I would have lost heart, unless I had believed That I would see the goodness of the LORD In the land of the living." (Psalms 27:13 NKJV). There is absolutely nothing wrong with expecting to see God's goodness while we are still alive on earth.

We are part of the generation that God is taking into the promise land. We do not enter into our promise with old mindsets. We allow God to deliver us from having a slave mentality by changing our thoughts in our wilderness. God uses our desert to give us to the proper mindset so that we can take possession of whatever He has for us.

We do not have to be afraid of the giants in the land. We do not have to fear our opposition because "If God be for us, who can be against us?" (Romans 8:31 KJV). It's business time!

My prayer is that God gives us peace in the midst of the storm. May God cause us to grow in His peace. May God help us to make the necessary changes to our lives while being empowered by His grace. Amen.

Chapter 6

The Pursuit of Joy

—————————————
· ● ·

One fruit of the Spirit that we may need to give a little more attention to in our discussions within Christian circles is joy. We find ourselves discussing peace and talking about love often. We rarely enter into dialogue about joy.

There is a significant distinction between having happiness and having the joy of the LORD. According to the Hebrew definition, joy can come from without or from within. For the purposes of this conversation, we will distinguish the two by calling one happiness and the other joy.

In my estimation, there are not too many people that do not have a desire to be happy. When we do not have a desire to be happy, then one could suggest that there may be something wrong with our psychosis. Most of us would love to be happy all day every day. We would love to be happy 24-7 with everything in our lives going well with no adversity as far as the eye can see. That would be amazing. Most of us would really enjoy that. Unfortunately, it is not realistic to expect a life without adversity.

There is a popular phrase which most of us are aware of, which is known as the 'pursuit of happiness.' "The pursuit of happiness is defined as a fundamental right mentioned in the Declaration of Independence to freely pursue joy and live life in a way that makes you happy, as long as you don't do anything illegal or violate the rights of others."

This is all well and good if we live simply by the laws of the United States government. As citizens of the Kingdom of God and as worshipers of the only true and living God, we live our lives from a different perspective.

There is nothing wrong with wanting to be happy. Nothing wrong with having a desire to be happy at all. Problems arise when we make happiness our pursuit. Why? Because happiness depends on favorable circumstances and/or conditions to survive.

All of us want to have a job that we always enjoy going to every day. All of us want to be in a marriage or be in a relationship with someone that we are considering to marry and always enjoy the company of that individual. All of us want children that never do anything wrong; where they never disappoint us or where we never have to correct them.

We desire to always enjoy the company of our family members or strangers for that matter and there never be any conflict. We have a desire to always enjoy the company of our brothers and sisters in

Christ and there to never be a disagreement. We really have these desires.

There is nothing wrong with having these desires. We should not however allow these desires to dictate how we think and allow our desire for happiness to control how we approach our lives and the people around us. Since always having favorable conditions will never be our reality, it can be our desire, but it should never be our pursuit.

Happiness can also be people dependent. For us to be happy when people are involved, those people need to always be in our favor. Those people also always have positive thoughts and words as it pertains to us.

When our pursuit is happiness, we become a manipulator of situations and worse, we become a manipulator of people. We have to create a favorable environment for ourselves and in order to do that, we have to always be in control. Since we have to be in control, we see people as objects or commodities and we do not see the value that God has placed in them.

We begin to use people for our purpose instead of seeing and understanding how people are a part of God's purpose. When we do not see people as a part of God's purpose, we do not help them to become more of what God would have them to be. On the contrary, we exploit them so that they become what we desire for them to be.

Because our happiness becomes more valuable than others, we manipulate others and control others for the sake of our own happiness. When we are the feeble-minded individual being controlled and exploited, we allow another individual to control us because we have placed more value on someone else's happiness over our own self-worth.

What we try to do is make someone that is already miserable happy. We become miserable trying to make someone else happy. How are we going to make someone that is miserable happy when that person does not even know how to make themselves happy? We try to make someone that is insecure feel secure. What is that? What are we doing? The devil is a lie.

The pursuit of our own happiness or the pursuit of someone else's happiness is dysfunctional. It can be very destructive to self and others. It can also destroy relationships which is something that God never intends.

The pursuit of our own happiness or the pursuit of someone else's happiness can also destroy our purpose. When we wait for favorable conditions or when we wait for someone who is around us to be happy to make a move, we never move into the purpose that God has for us. We also most certainly never move into our God given destiny.

Consequently, we have to wait for the people around us to be in agreement with what God told us to do when the people around us may not be hearing from the God that we serve. We have to wait until our financial situation turns around in order for us to move into our purpose. We have to wait for it to stop raining and for the sun to start shinning to make a move. The devil is another lie.

"He who observes the wind will not sow, And he who regards the clouds will not reap. As you do not know what is the way of the wind, Or how the bones grow in the womb of her who is with child, So you do not know the works of God who makes everything. In the morning sow your seed, And in the evening do not withhold your hand; For you do not know which will prosper, Either this or that, Or whether both alike will be good." (Ecclesiastes 11:4-6 NKJV).

When we check it out, the God that we serve made the sun and the rain. We need both to grow. We need the people who are on our side to grow, and we need the people who are against us to grow. We just have to receive and hold on to the revelation that "if God be for us, who can be against us?" (Romans 8:31b KJV). Who is greater than our God? Nobody!

Our pursuit then is going to be the Joy of the LORD. "The joy of the LORD is your strength." (Nehemiah 8:10b NKJV). The joy of the LORD is what gives us the strength to handle adverse circumstances and the people we find difficult in our lives who are in opposition to us.

Joy is described as having exuberance, elation, jubilation, delight, or great pleasure. The joy of the LORD is not really an emotion even though it may be expressed emotionally. We may sing, we may dance, or we may shout unto the LORD; but it is not about what's going on in our emotions. It is really about the elation that is going on in our spirits. It is elation, jubilation, delight, or great pleasure in who God is and who He is to us.

Our circumstances cannot give us this type of joy. Our situation cannot give us this type of joy. The people around us cannot give us this type of joy. Since the world does not give us this kind of joy then we are not going to allow the world to take our joy away from us.

The Word of God and the Spirit of God controls our thoughts so that we may have joy. When God's Word and His Spirit are not controlling our thoughts, our circumstances and people will control our thoughts. Consequently, this will cause us to believe that there is no hope and it will also cause us to feel defeated. We naturally will pursue happiness because we will seek to escape our adversity.

God wants our thoughts. We should allow Him to have our thoughts. Especially when it seems as if there is nothing going right in our lives.

The joy of the LORD comes through prayer, communion, and fellowship with the LORD. There is not a substitute for spending time with God. The joy of the LORD is not something we earn. The joy of the LORD is something we receive from fellowship with Him.

It very easy in this life to become distracted. It is so easy in life to have our focus stolen by what is going on around us. The joy of the LORD is something that we consistently pursue.

For most of us, when we are completely honest and transparent, we would have to admit that we have not mastered this. But like Paul said, "… but I follow after" (Philippians 3:12b KJV). This is our pursuit. We follow after. We pursue the joy of the LORD because the joy of the LORD is our strength.

In the 51st Psalms, David writes after his sin with Bathsheba and prays, "Restore to me the joy of Your salvation, And uphold me by Your generous Spirit." (Psalms 51:12 NKJV). Doing something wrong, making a mistake, or stepping outside of the perimeters that God has set for our lives can definitely rob us of our joy.

When we are living in a way that is contrary to the way that God would have for us to live, we are without question going to struggle in our pursuit for the joy of the LORD. When we are living in a way that is contrary to the way that God would have for us to live, we are not going to enjoy the peace of God either.

Paul says this, "And do not grieve the Holy Spirit of God, by whom you were sealed for the day of redemption." (Ephesians 4:30 NKJV). Grief occurs anytime there is a separation in fellowship. When we lose a love-one through death, we grieve. When we lose a spouse through divorce, we grieve. When we lose a friendship over irreconcilable differences, we grieve. When we are living in a way that is contrary to the way that God would have us to live, we grieve.

When we have the Spirit of God in us, we can experience being out-of-balance with Him. We will then feel the separation in our fellowship with Him. Grief is occurring because our sin has caused our fellowship with God to be severed. When we are grieving because of our out-of-balance with God, He is grieving as well.

We are going to struggle with having the joy of the LORD in our spirits when we are in involved in things that our destructive to self and others. We are going to struggle with having the peace of God when are not functioning correctly in our thinking. Because God's Spirit resides in us, the grief that we are experiencing is what God uses to correct our thinking and to bring us back into fellowship with Him.

An out-of-balance with God can also be caused by doing something constructive. We can become consumed with work because of the benefits or the rewards that we can reap. The term workaholism was coined in 1971 by minister and psychologist Wayne Oates, who described workaholism as "the compulsion or the uncontrollable need to work incessantly." We should have balance in our lives. God does not want us worshiping our work. God wants us to worship Him.

We cry out to God for His grace and for His mercy. We cry out to our Heavenly Father for His compassion that does not fail and for His favor that we know we do not deserve. God delivers us and restores the joy of our salvation.

God restores the joy from just knowing Him and having communion with Him. God restores the joy of being delivered and set free. God restores the joy of Jesus cleansing us with His own blood and for rising from the dead so that we may stand justified before Him. 'Father may You restore the joy of knowing that even though our situation seems out of control, that our life is in Your hands.'

The joy of the LORD gives us an assurance that even though we may be in the middle of a trial, we count it all joy because we know that, "No weapon formed against you shall prosper." (Isaiah 54:17a NKJV). We count it all joy because we know trouble does not last always. We count it all joy because we know this too shall pass.

We are not oblivious to our trial. We acknowledge the trial. We just know that our trials are not working against us; our trials are working for us. We count it joy because we know our tribulation is working perseverance, endurance, mental resilience and intestinal fortitude.

We need endurance because our transformation is not a sprint. We need endurance because our transformation is a marathon. "The race is not to the swift, Nor the battle to the strong." (Ecclesiastes 9:11 NKJV). We receive victory because of our endurance. When we come out of our trial we will be stronger, wiser, mature and complete.

"My brethren, count it all joy when you fall into various trials, knowing that the testing of your faith produces patience. But let patience have its perfect work, that you may be perfect and complete, lacking nothing." (James 1:2-4 NKJV).

Jesus says this, "These things I have spoken to you, that in Me you may have peace. In the world you will have tribulation; but be of good cheer, I have overcome the world." (John 16:33 NKJV) . Jesus has overcome the world and in Him we have the victory.

We are overcomers through Him. We are more than conquerors through Him. "For in him we live, and move, and have our being." (Acts 17:28a KJV). We make the necessary changes to our lives with the joy of the LORD. We better ourselves and the lives of others with the joy of the LORD.

Our battle is with seeking external things to give us joy. This type of joy or commonly known as happiness is temporary. It will not last long at all. It comes and goes. It is here today and gone tomorrow. The joy we need to sustain us and to give us strength for our lives comes from fellowship with Christ Jesus.

My prayer for us is that we delight ourselves in the LORD. My prayer for us is that we make the LORD our delight and not anything external. May our delight be Christ Jesus. As we delight ourselves in Him, God said He will give us the desires of our heart.

Sometimes hearing God's voice is a challenge because our desires override His voice. The closer we get to Him, the more our desires become like His. As we begin to pray His will, we discover that His will for us is better for us than our own will.

His will is better for us any day of the week and twice on Sundays. As we begin to desire what He desires, these are the desires that He fulfills. May the LORD multiply our joy. Amen.

Chapter 7

We Need Your Righteousness

One of the biggest deterrents to our walk with God is self-righteousness. Some may say one of the biggest deterrents, but if we were to ask God, He might say it is the biggest. A deterrent is defined as a thing that discourages or is intended to discourage someone from doing something. Our own self-righteousness can actually hinder the move of God in our lives. It can become a major roadblock in our path to fellowship with Him.

Self-righteousness is very destructive and very dangerous. It is destructive and dangerous because it is so deceptive. When we are self-righteous, we are spiritually blind. We are unaware of our own blindness. Other people can see it on us, but we do not recognize that we have it.

The Word of God is what is required to remove the blindfold and it requires self-evaluation. We begin by using God's Word to evaluate ourselves instead of using the Scriptures to evaluate others.

Our prayer becomes, 'LORD help us! LORD have mercy on us! Help us to see ourselves! LORD help me to see me!'

The Word of the LORD says this, "Judge not, that you be not judged. For with what judgement you judge, you will be judged; and with the measure you use, it will be measured back to you." (Matthew 7:1-2 NKJV). These are the Words of our LORD and Savior Jesus Christ. He tells us not to judge less we be judged. The same standard we use to measure others will be the same standard that He will use to measure us when we stand before Him.

Now, there ain't no way (excuse my use of poor English); but there ain't no way that we are going be able to stand before God and He give us eternal life, if He measures us the same way we measure others. When we are self-righteous, we measure others with a judgmental attitude and with a condescending disposition. If God uses the same ruler on us that we use on others, then we will not be able to stand before Him.

Why is this true? "For all have sinned and fall short of the glory of God." (Romans 3:23 NKJV). Also, "If You, LORD, should keep an account of our sins and treat us accordingly, O LORD, who could stand [before you in judgment and claim innocence]?" (Psalms 130:3 AMP). In essence, we have done too much dirt to qualify ourselves according to our own standard.

The truth of the matter is that we were disqualified from qualifying ourselves before Him before we have done anything wrong. David said this, "Behold, I was brought forth in iniquity, And in sin my mother conceived me." (Psalms 51:5 NKJV). We were born in sin. We were disqualified when we were born because sin was passed down to us from the first man Adam.

When we begin to comprehend the grace of God, it is a wonder how we could ever become self-righteous. Maybe this is our problem. We become self-righteous because we do not comprehend or understand His grace.

We cannot qualify ourselves before God with anything that we do. Weeks, months, or years of celibacy, sobriety, or fidelity does not bring us to a place where we are able to stand before Him. "But we are all like an unclean thing, And all our righteousnesses are like filthy rags; We all fade as a leaf, And our iniquities, like the wind, Have taken us away." (Isaiah 64:6 NKJV).

God equates our righteousness with that as of a filthy rag. A filthy rag in this particular text is not a cloth that has been used to wash the dishes. A filthy rag in this text is not a cloth that we use to wash our car or a cloth that has been used to take a bath. These cloths are reusable. A filthy rag in this particular text of Scripture is a cloth that has been used by a woman while on her menstrual cycle. It is something that is regarded as un-reusable.

From a husband's point of view, if his wife tried to offer her husband a used menstrual cloth as a token of her love for him; or she tried to use her used menstrual cloth to justify why they should be married to each other, under normal circumstances the husband is going to want to have his wife undergo a psychological evaluation.

We are going to be hard-pressed to find a husband who is not going to have some questions for his wife. Those questions could sound a little something like this: 'What do you want me to do with that? Throw it away for you? Flush it down the toilet? This is supposed to justify your love for me?'

That is the same way God sees our self-righteousness. Christ is our groom and we are His bride. God says this, "No weapon formed against you shall prosper, And every tongue which rises against you in judgment You shall condemn. This is the heritage of the servants of the LORD, And their righteousness is from Me,' Says the LORD." (Isaiah 54:17 NKJV). Our righteousness comes from the LORD.

To have righteousness with God means to be in right-standing with Him. The righteousness of God is not something we earn. The righteousness of God is a gift that we receive. Because we have right standing with Him, we do not make decisions predicated on public opinion. We reject every word that uses our past as a weapon against us and attempts to declare us guilty before God.

Why? Because our righteousness is not predicated on what we did or what we did not do. Our righteousness is predicated on what God did for us through the expressed image of His Person, which is Christ Jesus.

For us to have right-standing with God, the penalty for sin has to be satisfied. Celibacy does not satisfy the penalty for sin. Fidelity does not satisfy the penalty for sin. Neither does sobriety.

For some reason when we reference sin, we only like to discuss the 'three big sins'; fornication, adultery, and alcohol and substance abuse. As if these are the only sins that can be committed. Iniquity is deeper than that. Iniquity is a mystery. God has to reveal to us the mystery of iniquity.

"For the wages of sin is death." (Romans 6:23a KJV). The penalty for sin is only paid for through death. Death is the only thing in God's eyes that can satisfy the penalty for our sins. Someone has to die.

We have two choices. Either we can pay the price through death which will take us an eternity to do; or we can put our trust in the One who paid it all. Jesus died on the cross and shed His blood to satisfy God's judgment of sin against us. Why pay for something that has already been paid for? Why pay for something when you can get it for free? Salvation is free for us but it cost God something. It cost Him His only begotten Son in whom He was well pleased.

Salvation is personal. Salvation is personal because it is available to the entire world but unfortunately sometimes salvation is rejected. Salvation is not something we earn. Salvation is a gift that we receive. "For by grace you have been saved through faith, and that not of yourselves; it is the gift of God, not of works, lest anyone should boast." (Ephesians 2:8-9 NKJV).

Jesus carried the sins of the world; but as individuals we put our trust in the sacrifice that God provided. As believers, God takes our sins or our unrighteousness and places it on His Son Jesus the

Righteous One. He then takes the righteousness of His Son and gives it to us.

We understand that God has principles called laws that have to be fulfilled. His rules have to be followed. Someone had to walk within the perimeters of His Word. Someone had to 'dot every i and cross every t'. Since that is something we could not do, God did it for us though His Son.

We as believers trade places with Jesus. He took what we deserve and gives us what we do not deserve. "So that whoever believes and trusts in Him [as Savior] shall not perish, but have eternal life." (John 3:16b AMP).

"But He was wounded for our transgressions, He was bruised for our iniquities; The chastisement for our peace was upon Him, And by His stripes we are healed. (Isaiah 53:5 NKJV).

We do not have to bruise ourselves over our iniquities; and we do not have allow other people to bruise us over our iniquities either. We do not have to wound ourselves over our transgressions and we do not have to allow other people to wound us over our transgressions. The chastisement for our peace with God is not upon us. The chastisement for our reconciliation with God was upon Him; and with His stripes we decree and we declare that we are restored.

His blood was shed so that we might have a relationship with Him and be spiritually restored. We have reconciliation, justification, righteousness, and redemption through the death and resurrection of His Son Jesus. We have been redeemed or purchased by His own blood.

We belong to God because of our confidence in what He has done for us. We receive a gift. We cannot take credit for receiving a gift. We give the credit to the Giver of the Gift. All the credit, or all the glory belongs to our God.

The exchange of righteousness to us and of unrighteousness to Christ Jesus is what sent Him to the cross. While on the cross, "And about the ninth hour Jesus cried out with a loud voice, saying 'Eli, Eli, lama sabachthani?' that is, 'My God, My God, why have You forsaken Me?'" (Matthew 27:46 NKJV). He was forsaken because the sins of the world were upon Him.

Jesus was asking a rhetorical question. He was asking a question that does not require a response. Jesus was marveling at the love that God has towards us.

"Who shall separate us from the love of Christ? Shall tribulation, or distress, or persecution, or famine, or nakedness, or peril, or sword? Yet in all these things we are more than conquerors though Him who loved us. For I am persuaded that neither death nor life, nor angels nor principalities nor powers, nor things present nor things to come, nor height nor depth, nor any other created thing, shall be able to separate us from the love of God which is in Christ Jesus our LORD." (Romans 8:35,37-39 NKJV).

We are loved by Him. As believes we operate from a position of right-standing with God. Righteousness speaks to justification. We do not justify ourselves before God because of what we do. We justify ourselves before Him because of our faith in how merciful He is.

We justify ourselves before God because of our confidence in His death and resurrection. We are declared righteous because of the blood that Jesus shed. We are justified because Jesus got up out of the grave.

Self-righteousness may bring justification before men and women; but not before God. God's mercy and His grace brings us justification. Therefore, we are justified by faith in Christ Jesus. Those of us that are justified by God live by faith in His mercy. Those of us that are justified by God live by faith in His un-merited favor.

Paul put it this way; "For I am not ashamed of the gospel of Christ, for it is the power of God to salvation for everyone who believes, for the Jew first and also for the Greek (Gentile). For in it the righteousness of God is revealed from faith to faith; as it is written, "The just shall live by faith." (Romans 1:16-17 NKJV). God continues to reveal His righteousness to us as we continue to trust Him.

We are the righteousness of God in Christ Jesus. As a process we are growing in God to become more like Him. This speaks to the development of our character. As it pertains to having right-standing before God and having access to Him, we have that because of our faith in His blood and in His resurrection.

We are not driven or motivated to follow a set of regulations. This is where we try to justify ourselves before God by following rules. Jesus followed the rules for us. He has set us free from the law of sin and death.

When we try to follow the rules, it works death in us. When we follow Christ by walking in His Spirit, it works life in us. Walking in the Spirit is the equivalent of walking in love.

"But now we have been delivered from the law, having died to what we were held by, so that we should serve in the newness of the Spirit and not in the oldness of the letter." (Romans 7:6 NKJV). "For the letter kills, but the Spirit gives life." (II Corinthians 3:6b NKJV). "But he is a Jew who is one inwardly; and circumcision is that of the heart, in the spirit, not in the letter; whose praise is not from men but from God." (Romans 2:29 NKJV).

"Now the purpose of the commandment is love from a pure heart, from a good conscience, and from sincere faith." (I Timothy 1:5 NKJV). When we love God we keep His commandments because as we mature in God, we view sin as poison and not pleasure. We love God not as an emotion but we love Him as a decision. When we decide to love God we will obey Him. Amen.

When we deal with self, it qualifies us in the eyes of the LORD to handle others. It is not our gift or our talent that qualifies us in the eyes of God to handle His people. It is humility and compassion for others that qualifies us to handle God's people. It is our character.

When we are hurting we should not be in ministry. Positions of leadership in ministry is not for hurting people. Positions of leadership in ministry is for healed people. Why? Because hurt people, hurt people and healed people, help people.

We must learn how to deal with our own issues before we try to help someone else with theirs. My prayer for us is that we put our trust in God's righteousness so that we can grow and become more like Him. My prayer for you and I is that we love God, we love ourselves, and we love one another. Amen.

Chapter 8

Our Adversary

———————————
⋅ ● ⋅

There are a lot of lies out there about Satan. Ironically, they are all orchestrated by him. Satan puts the lies out there because he uses deception to disarm us. His lies are very strategic. We will not defeat him when we are unaware of how he operates. Paul wrote, "Lest Satan should take advantage of us; for we are not ignorant of his devices." (II Corinthians 2:11 NKJV). Satan uses ignorance to defeat us. He uses what we do not know to harm us.

"Be sober, be vigilant; because your adversary the devil walks about like a roaring lion, seeking whom he may devour." (1 Peter 5:8 NKJV). When we are not sober, then we cannot be vigilant. Sobriety and vigilance go hand and hand.

To be vigilant means keeping careful watch for possible danger of difficulties. To do this, we must remain sober or abstain from being under the influence of controlled substances. When we are under the influence of controlled substances, we make bad decisions to say the least.

When this book was initially written, it was written in first person. The intent was to have the reader evaluate themselves as opposed to those around them. To be effective and to achieve the results that God desires to achieve through this project, third person is a more effective approach. The goal is still the same and that is for us to evaluate ourselves, be reconciled to God, and to be unified as the Body of Christ.

The ultimate goal of this book is to allow God to repair our hearts and to help us His people to renew our minds. The title and overall theme of this project is 'LORD Help Me With Me'; because what was discovered was that we cannot renew our minds and achieve transformation until we cry out to God for help.

The overall desired objective to be achieved is for us to acquire and maintain proper perspective as we approach God, deal with self and handle others. It is very difficult however to talk about God and the things of God, and not to have anything to say about the common opponent that we all share. This particular chapter on our adversary the devil deals with the mindset we should have when we deal with him.

We have an adversary that we have to deal with. God does not want us to be afraid of Satan. When we are terrified of Satan, that terror comes from Satan himself. "For God has not given us a spirit of fear, but of power and of love and of a sound mind." (II Timothy 1:7 NKJV).

Our God does not distribute a spirit of fear, or of fright, or of terror. The spirit that our God distributes is a spirit of authority, of dominion or of power. He distributes a spirit of love, peace, and joy. Our God distributes a Spirit that stabilizes our heart and causes us to have a mind that is sound in judgment and decision making.

We are not going to focus on the false doctrines out there about Satan. If we were to dive into that, it might take us a lifetime to get to the truth. We will focus on the truth and how God wants us as followers of Him to think; and whatever false doctrines that Satan has filled our minds with about him may God set us free through His Word. "And you shall know the truth, and the truth shall make you free." (John 8:32 NKJV).

"For the weapons of our warfare are not carnal but mighty in God for pulling down arguments and every high thing that exalts itself against the knowledge of God, bringing every thought into captivity to the obedience of Christ, and being ready to punish all disobedience when your obedience is fulfilled." (II Corinthians 10:4-6 NKJV).

Our battle with Satan occurs in the mind. The mind is the battleground. Satan wants to control our thoughts through our senses. He uses what we can see physically, what we hear physically, what we touch, taste, and smell to dominate us.

He has not changed much if at all in his approach. This is the same approach that he used when he was able to dominate Adam and Eve in the Garden of Eden. When we want to know how Satan operates in the earth, there are two passages of Scripture that serve as a foundation.

The third chapter of Genesis is one and the fourth chapter of Matthew is the other. What we discover is that Satan entices us through the evil desires that are in our own sinful nature. Those evil desires when fulfilled, ultimately cause us to not only hurt ourselves but other people as well.

In the third chapter of Genesis we are introduced to Satan. "Now the serpent was more cunning than any beast of the field which the LORD God had made. And he said to the woman, 'Has God indeed said, 'You shall not eat of every tree of the garden'?'" (Genesis 3:1 NKJV). Satan begins by having us question what God has said. In order for us to walk with God we have to trust Him. Satan brings up questions in our minds to introduce doubt.

We should always trust God. Satan uses our physical senses to grab our attention in an attempt to take our focus off of our God and His Word. We do not access God through our physical senses. We access God through faith in His Word.

Our relationship with God is not physical at all. Our relationship with God is totally and completely spiritual. For us to have relationship with God, we have to trust what He says. Satan asks us questions in an attempt to get us to doubt our God.

Satan uses what we are connected to through our physical senses. He uses adverse circumstances, negative people, what we are attracted to or who we are attracted to introduce doubt in our minds. If Satan can get us off our square and cause us not to stand on God's Word, he will have his way with us.

The devil cannot make us sin but he sure can make things very enticing. What he does is make a presentation of evil; he presents something or someone that God says we cannot have or presents something that God says we should not do. We have to have a desire for what Satan offers or it is not a temptation.

Satan does not use what we do not want and who we do not want against us. He uses what we want and who we want against us. He uses our own evil desires against us in an attempt to kill, steal, and to destroy. "But each one is tempted when he is drawn away by his own desires and enticed." (James 1:14 NKJV).

After Satan gets us to question God, he then goes in for the kill by telling us more lies. He is so cunning. He is very persuasive. He is very patient.

"Then the serpent said to the woman, 'You will not surely die. For God knows that in the day you eat of it your eyes will be opened, and you will be like God, knowing good and evil.' So then the woman saw that the tree was good for food, that it was pleasant to the eyes, and a tree desirable to make one wise, she took of its fruit and ate. She also gave to her husband with her, and he ate." (Genesis 3:4-6 NKJV).

Our battle with Satan is in the mind. The situation and circumstances are very real. To overcome Satan, we must win the war that is going on in our minds. If Satan can get us to question God, consequently doubting Him, then our behavior will follow who and what we believe because we are losing the battle in our minds.

In life, we have two choices. "See, I have set before you today life and good, death and evil." (Deuteronomy 30:15 NKJV). Satan's objective is destruction. His mission is to kill, to steal and to destroy our lives. On the other hand, God offers us life. Jesus says, "I have come that they may have life, and that they may have it more abundantly." (John 10:10b NKJV).

As for Adam and Eve, the rest is history. We have been born into sin because we have inherited a sin nature from Adam who was the first man. Quick side note before we move on. We always talk about the tree of knowledge of good and evil but we never talk about the tree of life that was also in the garden.

There were two significant trees in the garden. "And out of the ground the LORD God made every tree grow that is pleasant to the sight and good for food. The tree of life was also in the midst of the garden, and the tree of the knowledge of good and evil." (Genesis 2:9 NKJV).

It is human nature for us to always focus on what we cannot have and what we cannot do; and to give little attention to what we can have and to what we can do. "No temptation has overtaken you except such as is common to man; but God is faithful, who will not allow you to be tempted beyond what you are able, but with the temptation will also make the way of escape, that you may be able to bear it." (I Corinthians 10:13 NKJV).

The LORD has provided a way of escape. When we are tempted, God will always make a way of escape for us. We do not have to decide to sin.

The LORD provided a way of escape for Adam and Eve. The Tree of Life was in the garden also. God never said before they had disobeyed Him that they could not partake of the Tree of Life. God only said that they could not partake of the tree of the knowledge of good and evil.

What if Adam and Eve would have called on God while they were being tempted and asked Him for help? Did they not know He was good? They had fellowship with Him. They were living in His goodness. They saw the wonder and splendor of God's creation.

Every one of Adam and Eve's needs were supplied. They had dominion and authority. If they had cried out to God, He would have shown them the way of escape that He had already prepared.

We should call on the LORD when we are being tempted. He is gracious enough to help us. God is merciful enough and gracious enough to help us with whatever temptation Satan throws our way. God will provide a way of escape.

"Let no one say when he is tempted, 'I am tempted by God'; for God cannot be tempted by evil, nor does He Himself tempt anyone." (James 1:13 NKJV). God is not tempting us. Satan is tempting us. He comes to tempt us so he can steal what God has given us. Satan comes to steal our purpose, take our destiny, and steal the dominion and authority we have been given. The devil is a lie, and the truth is not in him.

We should call on God and kneel before His throne of grace and mercy when we are in a situation or being tempted with something we cannot handle on our own. God will lead us to the Tree of Life. Jesus is the Tree of Life. God will make a way of escape so that we may be able to bear the temptation. Amen.

Now when we go to the fourth chapter of Matthew, and we see how Jesus (The Second Adam) handled temptation after forty days of fasting in the wilderness we see a totally different scenario. We should take a look at this particular text when given the opportunity (See Matthew 4:1-11 NKJV). Totally different isn't, it? Jesus used the Word of God to overcome the enemy because of the mindset He had.

Quoting or reciting Scripture only works when we believe it. The Word of God works when it is hidden in our hearts. "For with the heart one believes unto righteousness, and with the mouth confession is made unto salvation." (Romans 10:10 NKJV). It is the Word that is in our hearts that we use to overcome the wicked one.

The Word in the heart is what changes our thoughts. Memorizing Scripture only, is not effective in overcoming Satan. The devil knows scripture too. That is why we can preach the Scriptures, sing the Scriptures, and teach the Scriptures and Satan have is way with us.

We can memorize Scripture but to be effective we have to internalize Scripture. God's Word and the correct interpretation of His Word has to become a part of who we are. David said to God, "Your Word I have hidden in my heart, that I might not sin against You." (Psalms 119:11 NKJV).

It is the Word that is hidden in our hearts that changes our thoughts and our thoughts dictate how we converse and how we behave. The way Jesus handled Satan in his hour of temptation is the mindset that God wants us to have. God wants us to have the mind of Christ. He wants us to see sin as destructive. He wants us to use the Word of God to defend ourselves against the attack of the enemy who is coming against our minds.

The LORD is bringing us to a place of self-evaluation in order for us to view God correctly, see ourselves properly, and see others accurately. God also desires that we place more significance on Him and less significance on what we are going through; so that we can overcome whatever is going on in our lives. We need God to help us to change our thoughts and we need to know that we are loved by God.

May God reveal to us how gracious and how merciful He is, and may He give us the Word of faith. May God give us peace that surpasses all understanding and may He give us joy unspeakable and full of His glory. May God show us that He is our righteousness and may He bring us to a place where we view life correctly.

We must have the love of God and the wisdom of God. Everyone that is in sin is not demon-possessed. There is a difference from being controlled demonically and just simply being carnal. Sometimes we are not demon-possessed, sometimes we are just carnally minded. May God give us the wisdom we need to discern the difference.

The subject of mental illness may be a sensitive topic for some but we have to broach it. This is personal for some of us, because some of us have people in our lives who we love dearly who suffer with this. Also for some of us, we have love ones who have suffered with mental illness and unfortunately they are no longer with us.

Science has its proper place in society and modern-day medicine has its place in our society; but we also know Jesus to be a Deliver and a Healer. "If any of you lacks wisdom, let him ask of God, who gives to all liberally and without reproach, and it will be given to him." (James 1:5 NKJV). Every situation involving mental illness is different. Let us ask God for wisdom as it pertains to our own particular situations.

This war that we have with Satan is not physical. It's spiritual. "For we do not wrestle against flesh and blood, but against principalities, against powers, against the rulers of the darkness of this age, against spiritual hosts of wickedness in the heavenly places. Therefore, take up the whole armor of God, that you may be able to withstand in the evil day, and having done all, to stand." (Ephesians 6:12,13 NKJV).

When one of our brothers or our sisters has any struggle at all, they are having a wrestling match in their mind. If God has made us strong, instead of looking at them with a critical eye, maybe we should bear their infirmity. We bear our brother and sisters' weakness by praying for them and encouraging them.

We can also instruct them with grace and lead them to God's mercy. Unfortunately, some of us understand all too well how this is much easier said than done. Nevertheless, "We then who are strong ought to bear with the scruples of the weak, and not to please ourselves." (Romans 15:1 NKJV).

Satan wants to divide us. God desires for us to be reconciled to Him and to have unity with one another. Our adversary is not each other. We are not adversaries. Our adversary is Satan. May the LORD help us to walk in Kingdom principles as it relates to the prince of darkness; so that we are not tossed to and fro by every wind of doctrine that comes our way.

LORD help us to stand boldly knowing that You Father have given us authority over the enemy. We are not supposed to be running from him. He is supposed to be running from us. Bishop Noel Jones says this, "Satan does not belong in our face; he belongs under our feet." May the knowledge of God, His mercy, His peace, and His understanding be with us all. Amen.

Chapter 9

Walking In Victory

*W*henever we are in pursuit of a new job, one of the first things that we are inquisitive about are the wages. What will we be making? What are we going to earn? When it comes to sin, how come we never ask that question? When we are being tempted to do something, we know we have no business doing, why don't we ask, 'What is the wage?' What are we earning? If we were to ask God this very critical question, He would tell us that "the wages of sin is death." (Romans 6:23 KJV).

When our carnality is screaming at us to be satisfied, we do not see death. We do not see poison. What we see is pleasure or temporary gratification. We thought when we received God's Spirit that we would no longer have the desire to do evil. As we continue to walk with God, we find out the more we want to live right, the more we have a desire to live wrong.

We discover that even though we belong to God, and even though we have a desire to please God, that our sinful desires are still present with us. We want to do what is right, we know the difference between right and wrong, we have God's Spirit living on the inside of us, and we still desire to practice evil. "O wretched man that I am! Who will deliver me from this body of death?" (Romans 7:24 NKJV).

With all that going on, we take a look at God's law and we see how good God's Word is. We see that God's Word is good. We see that God's commands and His instructions are for our benefit. We see that His law is constructive. We see that God's Word makes our life better and how His law is for our protection. God's Word is not our problem. God's law is holy, just, and good.

"We know that the Law is spiritual, but I am a creature of the flesh [worldly, self-reliant - carnal and unspiritual], sold into slavery to sin [and serving under its control]." (Romans 7:14 AMP). We are the problem because we are carnally minded and sold into slavery to sin. We are the problem because we are sensual. We are the problem because we are controlled by sensual appetites, sensual habits, and sensual desires.

The way we think is carnal. Our behavior and our conversation is carnal. We have desires that are in direct opposition to God and we sometimes act on those desires. We are a mess. We are truly a mess.

We are gifted, but we are carnally minded. We are articulate, but we are carnally minded. We are fearfully and wonderfully made, but we are still carnally minded. Paul asks the question, "Who will deliver me from this body of death?" (Romans 7:24b NKJV).

We have spent years attempting to please God by attempting to keep His commandments to no avail. We have spent years trying to live right to gain His approval. We have spent years trying to live right so we could have eternal life. What we have learned and what we are still learning is that His approval cannot be earned.

What we are finding out is that we are saved by God's grace and His mercy. We are beginning to discover that without faith in His grace and mercy, it is impossible to please Him. For us to please God, we have to believe that He is who He says He is; and that He will reward us when we seek Him.

We do not please God to gain His acceptance. We please Him because we are already accepted by Him. "To the praise of the glory of His grace, by which He made us accepted in the Beloved." (Ephesians 1:6 NKJV).

We have two different and distinct mentalities. We have a carnal mind and we have a spiritual mind. Our carnal mind is controlled by sensual perception. What we see controls us. What we hear controls us. What we touch controls us. What we smell controls us. What we taste controls us.

Our carnal mind which is influenced by a wicked heart, makes decisions dictated by how we feel and by how we are connected to the world around us and the people in it. People especially play a significant role; because when we are carnally minded, the people that we have given significance to will have a negative impact on how we think. The sad part about it is that we can allow people to have a negative impact on how we think and feel about ourselves.

This is a very dangerous and a counter-productive way to live our lives. This is very destructive. "For to be carnally minded is death." (Romans 8:6a KJV). It is dangerous to allow others who are not being influenced by God to influence our decision making. When we allow ourselves to be controlled by a carnal mentality, we will destroy ourselves. When we live our lives dictated by our evil heart and the evil heart of negative people, we will die spiritually. The question now becomes; How can we be set free or how can we live the way God would have us to live?

God desires to bring us to a place where we are held accountable by Him and only Him. "The eyes of the LORD are in every place, beholding the evil and the good." (Proverbs 15:3 KJV). There is no man that can be with us 24-7. God is with us 24-7.

God desires to bring us to a place where walking with Him is not about following a set of rules. Walking with God is about growing in love with Him. We only love God when we are convinced that we are loved by Him. God loves us forever. He loves us with an everlasting love. We love Him because He first loved us.

His love for us is proved by the enormous sacrifice that He provided. God would not have given us such an enormous sacrifice if He did not love us. God did not wait until we got ourselves together before He provided this enormous sacrifice. God provided this sacrifice when we were a mess and did not have the capacity or the capability to love Him in return.

We grow in love with His sacrifice. We grow in love with His mercy. We grow in love with His grace. When we grow in love with God and we deny ourselves and follow Him.

When we are carnally minded, we do not see God's grace properly. When we are carnally minded and when we have not learned how to deny ourselves, we see the grace of God as a license or as liberty to be dysfunctional. When we are tempted we seek immediate gratification because we see sin as pleasure. When we are spiritually minded and being tempted with sin, we do not see pleasure; we see poison.

Paul says this, "What shall we say then? Shall we continue in sin that grace may abound?" (Romans 6:1 NKJV). God has given us an abundance of grace. He has given us an abundance of mercy. Because God has shown us so much mercy and so much grace, we sometimes think we have been liberated to indulge in our sinful nature.

Contrary to popular opinion, this is not how we are supposed to think. Sin is so destructive. Now, why would God give us an abundance of grace and an abundance of mercy so that we can continue to destroy ourselves and destroy others. God does not distribute grace to be destructive. He gives us grace so that we can exercise power over our destructive devices and so that we can walk victoriously.

Our prayer is that God gives us a spiritual mindset. We pray that we see our sin as destructive. We pray that we view our sin as dysfunctional. Our prayer is that we see our sin as poison and not pleasure. This is the mindset that God desires that we develop.

The blood that Jesus shed can reach us when we are on the mountain. The blood that He shed can also reach us when we are in the valley of the shadow of death. God loves us. God loves us. God loves us. We love Him because He first loved us. We love ourselves because God loves us.

We destroy self with sin when we do not love ourselves. We receive God's love so that we can love Him, love self and love others. God loves us. The proof is in His sacrifice.

We are now learning how to live our lives according to a spiritual mindset. "But to be spiritually minded is life and peace." (Romans 8:6b KJV). When we are controlled by our spiritual mind we have life and peace.

Our carnal mind operates by sight. It is dictated by the thoughts and opinions of people. Our spiritual mind operates by faith in God. We connect to God by faith in His Word. "So then faith comes by hearing, and hearing by the Word of God." (Romans 10:17 NKJV). "For with the heart one believes unto righteousness, and with the mouth confession is made unto salvation." (Romans 10:10 NKJV).

God deposits His Word into our hearts. His Word saves us. His Word delivers us. His Word brings us out of our mess. The Word that God deposits in our hearts changes our thoughts and therefore alters our conversation and our confession.

We do not just believe that we will be saved. We believe that we are saved. We do not just believe that we will have eternal life. We believe that we have eternal life. Our conduct, our character, and our confession is a reflection of what we believe.

When we do not believe that we are saved, we will not live like we are saved. On the other hand, when we believe that we have eternal life, we will grow in character and conduct ourselves accordingly. It is all very psychological. "For as he (she) thinks in his (her) heart, so is he (she)." (Proverbs 23:7a NKJV).

The devil comes to make us believe that we are not saved when we make a mistake. That mistake then becomes perpetual or continual. When we make a mistake, we begin to believe that we do not belong to God and we continue to live a life of dysfunction that leads to our own demise. We begin to believe that we are condemned and instead of running to God we run from Him.

There is nothing that we go through that we cannot overcome. God will not put more on us than what we can bear. We are more than conquerors through Him that loves us. The power of God is in His mercy. Sometimes we put so much significance on the forgiveness of others and we reduce the significance or the importance of the forgiveness of God.

Whether others forgive us or not is insignificant as it pertains to us walking victoriously. We have a deep desire for others to forgive us because none of us desire to be rejected. As it pertains to our deliverance, the acceptance of others is not a necessity.

The forgiveness that we receive from others is for their healing only and not for ours. Receiving forgiveness from others is a necessary component in reconciling a relationship and an apology can help to assist that. Receiving forgiveness from others however is our desire; but it is not necessary for us to have to walk victoriously.

The important thing, the principal thing, the most significant thing is that we receive forgiveness from God. When we receive God's mercy we can forgive ourselves and we are empowered to move on with the rest of our lives. Do we want others to forgive us? Sure, absolutely because oftentimes we desire reconciliation; but our lives do not have to be held hostage by someone's unwillingness to forgive us. "If God be for us who can be against us?" (Romans 8:31b KJV).

God desires that we live our lives by faith in Him. He desires that we live our lives continually and perpetually confident in His grace and mercy. God is bringing us to the place where we are reducing the significance of the opinions of others and increasing the significance of what God has to say to us and about us.

His Word comes to help us change our mind. He is bringing us to a place of victorious living. God wants us to have a mind where we trust that we belong to Him. We have been purchased by His blood and we have been adopted into His Kingdom.

What God wants to accomplish for us is that we put to death the sin that is at work in our lives. God wants us to deny ourselves so that we can have fellowship with Him. God wants us to no longer view sin as pleasure but view it as dysfunctional and destructive.

God wants us to deny ourselves so that He can reveal Himself to us. God wants us to deny ourselves so we can have life and have it in abundance.

The intent and purpose of God's commandments is love. To walk in the Spirit is to walk in love. To walk in love is to walk in the Spirit. They are one in the same. God wants us to love Him, love ourselves and love one another as we love ourselves. When we love God, we will keep His commandments.

God does not want our confidence to be in our ability to follow a set of rules. God wants our confidence in Him. He wants our thoughts to be perpetually connected to His grace and mercy. When we are babes in Christ, we see grace and mercy as liberty to sin. As we begin to grow and mature in God, we see grace as dominion over sin.

May the LORD free us from people who try to put a rush on the timetable that He has set for our transformation. This timetable is set by God and not by others. "My son, do not despise the chastening of the LORD, Nor be discouraged when you are rebuked by Him; For whom the LORD loves He chastens, And scourges every son (child) whom He receives" (Hebrews 12:5,6 NKJV).

God is the one setting the timetable for our deliverance. He corrects us because He loves us. Just as a father or mother who loves their child and sees them as a future adult; a parent will correct their child because they do not want their child to harm themselves. The LORD's correction can be grievous at times. Let us remain confident that His correction is out of His love for us and out of our own best interest.

God is correcting how we think because He loves us. God knows how to bring us out. God knows how to get us to change our mind. We have a will that God has chosen not to override. He will not change our mind, but because we belong to Him, He will get us to change our mind. Bishop Noel Jones said it like this, "Sometimes you almost have to lose your mind before you change your mind."

Sometimes our approach to our life is just off. There is really not a better way to put it. Sometimes our thinking is off. When our flesh is completely out of control, our mindset is that we are going to operate in our flesh this one last day or operate in it this one last time so we can get it out of our system. This is wrong.

Anything that we want to die we cannot continue to feed. Anything we want to die, we must starve. Why do we think we can get dysfunction out of our system by feeding it? The devil is a lie. We cannot continue to feed our flesh and expect it to die. When we are ready for the flesh to die, we have to starve it.

We have had many struggles in our lives. We have wrestled with many different things. From substance abuse to alcohol addiction, from sexual immorality to eating incorrectly and using money incorrectly. When we are honest with God and honest with ourselves we have to admit that we have struggled.

Fasting is good for spiritual strength because when we fast, we are humbling ourselves before the LORD. When we humble ourselves before God, He shows us His favor. God is not resisting us because of our sin. He is resisting us because of our pride. "God resists the proud, But gives grace to the humble." (James 4:6b NKJV).

In the past we have thought that fasting was to get God to move. What we are learning is God does not need to move. He is immutable. We are the ones that need to move.

John the Baptist said, "He (Jesus) must increase, but I must decrease." (John 3:30 KJV). We should get out of God's way and allow Him to perform the work that He wants to perform in our lives. Sometimes we can be standing in our own way and we can be our own worst enemy.

Pastor Bruce Parham has a song entitled "Hide Me." This song is a depiction of a worshiper who is petitioning the LORD to be hidden in God's glory. He is asking God to hide him from his worst enemy which is himself. Once we find out who we are in God, our worst enemy is not the devil. A majority of the time our worst enemy is ourselves.

"You will show me the path of life; In Your presence is fullness of joy; At Your right hand are pleasures forevermore." (Psalms 16:11 NKJV). What fasting does is it decreases our sinful nature and increases the presence of God in our spirits and in our thoughts.

Denying self requires being comfortable with being uncomfortable. It hurts to deny ourselves. It can be painful. The most challenging or the most difficult enemy to defeat in our lives is the enemy that we enjoy.

There are times in our lives where we can find ourselves in a cycle of relapse and recovery. A cycle where we find ourselves falling down and getting up. Let us remember the exhortation that says, "For a just man (woman) falleth seven times, and riseth up again." (Proverbs 24:16 KJV). "And we know that all things work together for good to those who love God, to those who are the called according to His purpose." (Romans 8:28 NKJV).

We may fall but we get up. We keep getting up until we learn how not to fall. We know the God who is able to sustain us in the cycle of relapse and recovery. This cycle however gets exhausting. Now let's know the same God who is able to keep us from falling.

"Now until Him that is able to keep you from falling, and to present you faultless before the presence of His glory with exceeding joy, To the only wise God our Saviour, be glory and majesty, dominion and power, both now and ever. Amen." (Jude 1:24,25 KJV).

LORD help us to be transformed from the inside-out and not the outside-in. Let your Word penetrate our hearts and renew our minds so we can be pleasing in your sight. Thank you Father for what you have done, what you are doing, and what you are going to do in our lives. We bless your holy name. It is in the name of Jesus we pray. Amen.

Chapter 10

LORD Teach Us To Pray

*L*earning how to pray is critical to our walk with God. Prayer is regarded as communication with our Heavenly Father. Our Father who is relational desires a relationship with us. When we pray incorrectly, it will hinder our communication with Him. In the sixth chapter of St. Matthew, our LORD and Savior Jesus Christ teaches us how to pray. We can also find in the eleventh chapter of St. Luke where our LORD teaches on prayer.

Prayer is predicated on the condition of our heart and the mindset that we have when we go into prayer. Our LORD teaches us how to pray by showing us in these chapters how we should think as it relates to Him, as it relates to self and as it relates to others.

When Jesus speaks to us, He wants His Word to move from our intellects to our hearts so it can change our thoughts. Our thoughts are not changed by the Word that is our intellect. Our thoughts are not changed by the Word that we have memorized or that we can recite. Our thoughts are changed by the Word that is hidden in our hearts. We can recite 'The LORD's Prayer,' but the real question is; Is 'The LORD's Prayer' hidden in our hearts?

At the beginning of the eleventh chapter of St. Luke, the disciples ask Jesus to teach them how to pray as John the Baptist taught his disciples to pray. Prayer is essential to the life of the believer. For any relationship to have survival, there must be communication. Without communication, all relationships will suffer tremendously.

Relationships break down because of a lack of communication. Prayer is communication between our Heavenly Father and us. That is all prayer really is. Prayer is not mystical. Prayer is spiritual. Prayer is communication. It is where we talk to God and God talks to us.

The more of God's Word that we have in our spirits the better. God does not respond to the Word that we have memorized. He responds to the Word that we have hidden in our hearts. Why? Because we have to have faith to access Him. Faith is not in our intellect but faith is in our hearts. "For with the heart one believes..." (Romans 10:10a NKJV).

'The LORD's Prayer' is designed to reset our hearts and recondition our minds as it relates to God and our world around us. Our request or our petition to God today is that He teach us how to pray and to encourage us to pray. Who wants to pray and not be heard? Who wants to pray and not be effective? Who wants to pray and not get a response? All of us want God to hear us when we call on Him.

"The effective fervent prayer of a righteous man avails much." (James 5:16b NKJV). As the LORD continues to reveal to us, our righteousness is not of ourselves; but our right-standing with God comes from Him. We have access to God through the blood the Son shed on Calvary and by His resurrection alone. Our righteousness does not give us access to Him. We only have access to God through His grace and mercy. His door is always open. We always have access to His throne as long as we put our confidence in the Son.

Our petition to God is LORD teach us how to be effective and fervent so that our prayers can avail much. Bishop Noel Jones said this, "much of prayer is repeating His Word back to Him. 'The LORD's Prayer', in the sixth chapter of St. Matthew is broken up into five verses. If we look a little bit deeper, we will see seven different sections.

"In this manner, therefore, pray: Our Father in heaven, hallowed be Your name. Your kingdom come. Your will be done on earth as it is in heaven. Give us this day our daily bread. And forgive us our debts, As we forgive our debtors, And do not lead us into temptation, But deliver us from the evil one. For Yours is the kingdom and the power and the glory forever. Amen." (Matthew 6:9-13 NKJV).

When we pray the Word of God from the heart, we are not necessarily praying in a specific order. There is not a specific format. It depends on the day. Each day is different. Jesus says, "In this manner, therefore, pray..." (Matthew 6:9a NKJV). What Jesus is saying is that we do not necessarily have to recite this passage of Scripture; but this should be our approach to God when we pray.

When we approach God, we should approach God with humility. We should approach Him with respect. We should also approach Him with thanksgiving.

We might ask for forgiveness first. We might ask for daily bread first. It depends on what is going on in our hearts. It depends on what is pressing on our minds. No matter what is pressing, we should always approach Him with humility, with respect, and with thanksgiving.

Our approach to Him is always the same. "Our Father in heaven..." (Matthew 6:9b NKJV). He is our Father. A very popular song, sung by Chris Tomlin called 'Good Good Father' is a depiction of how the condition our hearts and our minds should be when we approach Him. Another good song is 'Lord You Are Good' by Todd Galberth. When we listen to this song, we hear Todd Galberth's testimony on how he wrote this song during a difficult time in his life.

Sometimes our circumstances can be so adverse, and our situation can be so negative that it can literally rob us of our praise for God. We can begin to question God, or we can begin to find fault in Him. This can literally send us into despair and depression.

The devil wants our minds on our circumstances. He wants our minds on our situation so that we can define the goodness of the

LORD by how favorable or unfavorable our situation or circumstances are. The devil is a lie and the truth is not in him.

The goodness of the LORD cannot be defined by our circumstances. Our circumstances may be negative. In the midst of all that we are going through, we declare to God from our heart that, LORD You are good. "I will bless the LORD at all times; His praise shall continually be in my mouth." (Psalms 34:1 NKJV).

Todd Galberth put it like this: "LORD you are good. You've been so good. LORD you are good. You've been better than good. I can't praise you enough. I owe you my life. Can't praise you enough even if I try; because you've been, so good, to me."

Good gospel music is so important. I thank God for all the Gospel Music artists and musicians that are truly worshipers and who minister to us through song. Music is very powerful. The song in our hearts is actually part of our communication to God.

"Speaking to one another in psalms and hymns and spiritual songs, singing and making melody in your heart to the LORD." (Ephesians 5:19 NKJV). This is important. A good gospel song in our hearts can make the difference in how we think, how we approach our day, and how we approach our lives.

'LORD you are a good Father.' That's how we should approach Him. Our approach to God should be with thanksgiving. "...with thanksgiving, let your requests be made known unto God." (Philippians 4:6b NKJV).

Sometimes we are so discouraged that we need to read Scripture and play some good gospel music before we enter into His presence. Sometimes our spirits can be so depleted because our minds are on all the things that we may be going through or on what is going on around us.

God's Word and songs inspired by His Spirit release our thoughts from our situation and put them on Him. We approach God as our Father. As our Father, we seek Him for wisdom, for guidance, for counsel, for protection, and for provision.

"Hallowed be Your name." (Matthew 6:9c NKJV). Secondly, our confession to God is that His name is hallowed or that His name is scared. God's name is holy and above any other name that is named. His name is to be revered and to be respected.

When we believe that God is blessed, we believe that He is everlasting. When we believe that God is blessed, we believe that He is great. When we believe this, why would we ever take His name and couple it with a word that is the abbreviation for damnation?

Damnation means destruction or to demolish. When we believe His name is sacred, why would we use His name vainly or haphazardly? The devil is a lie. God is holy. God is eternal. God is blessed. Hallowed be Your name!

When we call on His name, it should always be with reverence. We should always hold the name of the LORD in high regard. LORD Jesus, forgive us for using your name in vain. Father have mercy on us. We receive Your mercy. Thank you. Holy be Your name!

"Your kingdom come. Your will be done On earth as it is in heaven." (Matthew 6:10 NKJV). In heaven, Jesus is King and LORD of all. On earth, we make Him King in our lives. On earth we make Him LORD over our circumstances, in our situations and in our relationships.

Many times in our hearts and in our thoughts, we give more significance to the people in our lives and the things going on in our lives than we do to the God that we serve. Sometimes we give more significance to people who could care less about us or whose love for us could never be equated to love that God has for us. God loves us more than we would ever know.

God reveals to us who or what we have made king of our hearts and of our thoughts. Whatever we have made king of our hearts and of our thoughts is controlling our life. When we pray, 'let Your Kingdom come, let Your will be done', we are requesting that Christ Jesus become King of our hearts and of our thoughts. We are asking that God become LORD over the decisions that we make. LORD we are requesting that we make You more significant than anyone or anything; so that You now can maneuver our lives.

'Let Your Kingdom come, let Your will be done' is also a petition for wisdom and order. When we have dysfunction, carouse, confusion and unnecessary foolishness going on in our lives, then we are in need God's Kingdom to come on earth. "For God is not the author of confusion but of peace." (I Corinthians 14:33a NKJV).

Our Father is in heaven. We are on earth. We need wisdom and order while on earth because we live in a world that is full of distractions. We pray that God's Kingdom reign in us because we need wisdom and order in our decision making.

We pray that God's Kingdom reign in our homes. We pray that God's Kingdom reign in our schools. We pray that God's Kingdom reign in our businesses, our ministries, and our places of employment. We pray that God's Kingdom reign in our government.

We pray that God's Kingdom reign in our marriages. We pray that God's Kingdom reign in our relationships with our parents and in our relationships with our children. We pray that God's Kingdom reign in our finances. We pray that God's Kingdom reign in the health of our bodies. We pray for God's wisdom and God's order for every particular situation pertaining to our lives.

This is a daily prayer. Father help us to pray more. Every day we are in a battle to walk victoriously. Not a single day should go by where we do not have communication with our Heavenly Father. Which brings us to section four. "Give us this day our daily bread." (Matthew 6:11 NKJV).

When Jesus was tempted by Satan in the wilderness after forty days of fasting, Jesus said to him, "It is written, 'Man shall not live by bread alone, but by every Word that proceeds out of the mouth of God.'" (Matthew 4:4 NKJV). God's Word is our food for our souls. Our souls need spiritual food daily in order to survive. God's Word works in concert with prayer.

God's Word is not tangible. God's Word is spiritual. He enlightens us spiritually. God reveals Himself to us.

When we read the Scriptures, we want to depend on the Spirit of God for the interpretation. When we read the Scriptures, we ask God for illumination. We read the Scriptures depending on His Spirit to turn on the light. God illuminates, brightens, or shines light on His Word; if not we will never view His Word correctly.

God does this for us daily. He turns on the light in our spirits. LORD, we need spiritual food for our hearts and for our thoughts.

"Your Word is a lamp to my feet, and a light to my path." (Psalms 119:105 NKJV). God's Word dictates the decisions that we make in our lives. God's Word is our flashlight when we are in a dark place. When we cannot see our way out; God's Word leads us out.

His Word is the flashlight for our feet. God's Word is light for our dark paths. His Word leads and guides us when there is nothing but darkness all around us. God's Word is daily nutrition for our souls. Father give us this day our daily bread. Amen.

LORD Teach Us To Pray Part II

"And forgive us our debts, as we forgive our debtors." (Matthew 6:12 NKJV). It is very well possible that our previous experiences were so adverse and were so traumatic that our thoughts are being controlled by the memory of our past. Satan's whole entire purpose is destruction. He comes to create havoc in order to leave us paralyzed psychologically.

Satan wants our hearts filled with bitterness, resentment, malice, revenge, and un-forgiveness. 'LORD, help us to see You even in the face of all that we have had to endure. Father, You said that You have come that we might have life and that we may have it in abundance. LORD we pray that You give us abundant life.'

Satan wants our hearts filled with un-forgiveness, so that we may have dysfunctional thoughts that lead to destructive behavior. 'We pray LORD that You set us free.' It is possible to be delivered from a negative situation, be delivered from an adverse circumstance, or delivered from a tumultuous relationship and still be controlled by the memory of it. The individual that Satan used to wound us has moved on and we are left here with all this baggage.

We refuse to forgive others because we see forgiveness as a weakness. We use un-forgiveness, bitterness, resentment, revenge and retaliation to protect ourselves. We see un-forgiveness as self-preservation. Unfortunately, un-forgiveness does not protect us. Un-forgiveness eats us alive and causes us to make decisions that ultimately hurt us long-term.

There is a difference between forgiveness and reconciliation. Sometimes we confuse the two. When we forgive, we release others of the debt that is owned to us from trespassing against us. When someone trespasses against us, they are indebted to us.

So that we can free ourselves, not necessary the other person, we forgive. We do not forgive so that we can be reconciled to the person that harmed us. We forgive so that we can heal. We use wisdom as it pertains to reconciling the relationship. Unfortunately, depending on the mitigating circumstances, some relationships are irreconcilable.

When we forgive, we are not weak. It does not require a lot of strength to retaliate. It does not require a lot of strength to be spiteful. It does not require a lot of strength to operate in un-forgiveness. Forgiveness requires strength. It requires strength to forgive. That means when we forgive, we are not weak. When we forgive it is because we are strong.

We ask God for forgiveness for our debts first. We ask God for forgiveness and we receive forgiveness. When we receive forgiveness, we do not forgive others first. When we receive forgiveness from God, we forgive ourselves first. When we receive forgiveness from God and when we forgive ourselves, we are then empowered to forgive others.

God wants us to take ownership of our lives. We do not own someone else's choices. We own our own choices. When people hurt us, that was not our decision. That was their decision. We take ownership of the decisions that we make because we can only change our decisions when we own them.

When we hold other people responsible for the decisions that we make, we give those people power over our choices. When we hold others responsible for our dysfunction, Satan will use those individuals to control our thoughts with a memory. To overcome that, we own our dysfunction, receive God's mercy for our dysfunction and we release it into God's hands. As we are being set free as a process, we receive God's grace so we can walk victoriously.

What sets us free is receiving forgiveness from God so that we can forgive ourselves. When we forgive ourselves, we are then empowered to forgive others. Our freedom is in forgiveness. We may never forget what happened but we do not have to be controlled by the memory of it. God reveals to us that forgiveness is necessary for survival. God is not asking us to forget. God is asking us to forgive so that we can heal. Let us decide to heal.

May God give us power by His mercy that he has shown us so that we are no longer controlled by the memory of the offense. Because of the blood that Jesus shed, and by His resurrection, the memory of the offense does not control us. We control the memory.

LORD, forgive us as we forgive one another. We pray LORD that You show us and teach us how to forgive. Also give us wisdom in the reconciliation of our relationships. Amen.

"And do not lead us into temptation, But deliver us from the evil one." (Matthew 6:13a NKJV). This particular Scripture gives us a lot of trouble because we cannot understand why God would require us to ask Him to not lead us into temptation. What we say to ourselves and to God is, 'LORD if you don't want us to be led into temptation just don't lead us into temptation. Why do we have to ask You not to be led into temptation?'

What we discover as it pertains to our relationship with God is that we are not robots. As we begin to mature in God, we learn that God has given us a will that He has chosen not to override. God chose us before the foundation of the world. This is predicated on the knowledge He has before the world began. We are chosen by God according to His foreknowledge.

God declares the end from the beginning, then works it out in time. He will not change our minds, but He will bring us to a place where we decide to change our minds. What is simply a consequence for most becomes chastening for us, His people. "For whom the LORD loves He chastens, And scourges every son whom He receives." (Hebrews 12:6 NKJV).

The LORD also said, "My sheep hear My voice, and I know them, and they follow Me." (John 10:27 NKJV). When we belong to God, we hear His voice even in valleys of our life. When we belong to God, we hear His voice even when we are in situations that we have no business being in. When we belong to God we hear His voice even when we are in the wrong place at the wrong time because, "My sheep hear My voice, and I know them, and they follow Me." (John 10:27 NKJV).

We begin to cry out to the LORD, 'I can't keep doing this! I can't keep living like this! LORD, help me! I need you to bring me out one more time!' We begin to receive the revelation of how deceitful and how desperately wicked our heart is and we realize if we are led by our own heart then we are not going to make it.

"Let no one say when he is tempted, 'I am tempted by God'; for God cannot be tempted by evil, nor does He Himself tempt anyone. But each one is tempted when he is drawn away by his own desires and enticed. Then, when desire has conceived, it gives birth to sin; and sin, when it is full-grown, brings forth death." (James 1:13-15 NKJV).

When we truly understand this passage of Scripture and this particular aspect of 'The LORD's Prayer as it pertains to temptation, we begin to pray every day for the rest of our lives: 'LORD I need you to lead me away from temptation. LORD I need you to lead me away from distractions. LORD I need you to lead my heart and I need you to help me to control my thoughts. LORD when I follow my heart, I find myself in situations that I know I don't have any business being in. LORD help me and lead me. Amen.'

Our walk with God requires faith in Him. It requires absolute trust. We are so vulnerable. All of us are. Our prayer to our Heavenly Father is also, "So teach us to number our days, That we may gain a heart of wisdom." (Psalms 90:12 NKJV).

Sometimes it takes us a while for us to receive the revelation of how much we need God. He is bringing us to a place of absolute trust in Him. We are getting to a place in our lives where we realize we are not going to make it unless we trust Him. "Oh, taste and see that the LORD is good; Blessed is the man who trusts in Him!" (Psalms 34:8 NKJV).

"For Yours is the kingdom and the power and the glory forever. Amen." (Matthew 6:13b NKJV). The Kingdom belongs to God. He has all authority and all the glory belongs to Him.

In America, where I am from, we live in a democracy. In a democracy, we have a president that presides over the country. In a democracy, there is freedom of speech, and we all have our own identity. God's government is not a democracy. God's government is a monarchy.

In a democracy, the people collectively with the government make the rules. In a monarchy or a kingdom, the king makes the rules. In the Kingdom of God, Jesus sits on the throne. The Kingdom belongs to Him. We are citizens of the Kingdom of God and we do not have our own identity. We take on the identity of our King.

Paul say this, "All things are lawful for me, but not all things are helpful; all things are lawful for me, but not all things edify." (I Corinthians 10:23 NKJV). As it pertains to our local governments; something may be legal to do as a citizen of the United States of America, but that does not necessary mean it is legal to do as a citizen of the Kingdom of God.

Just because local government says its legal, does not necessarily mean it is beneficial. Just because something is accepted by local society does not mean it is accepted by our King. If it is destructive to self and destructive to others and does not build us up as people, then our King does not accept it as legal.

As a citizen of God's Kingdom, we live by His standards. God's standards are higher than that of the United States government or any of other government of this world. We are called to live and walk with God in love. We submit to the One that is sitting on the throne in the Kingdom of God and that would be none other than Christ Jesus.

In Christ's first coming, He came as the 'Lamb of God' to take away the sins of the world. He is sitting on a throne of grace because He is orchestrating salvation to mankind. In Christ's second coming, He is coming as the 'The Lion of the Tribe of Judah' and He will be sitting on a throne of judgement. Jesus will gather His elect and execute judgment against those who reject Him and against those who are in opposition to Him. This is unfortunate but this has to be said.

Christ Jesus is the Lamb, and He is the Lion. He is our Savior and He is our Judge. He is to be adored, to be appreciated, and to be respected.

We submit to His grace now as Savior, so we will reign with Him later as our Judge. "This is a faithful saying: for if we died with Him, we shall also live with Him. If we endure, we shall also reign with Him. If we deny Him, He also will deny us." (II Timothy 2;11-12 NKJV).

There are two dispensations. There is the dispensation of grace and there is the dispensation of judgment. We have the opportunity to walk with God while He is gracious and merciful. When we refuse to accept His grace, we will be forced to accept His judgement.

Jesus says, "I must work the works of Him who sent Me while it is day; the night is coming when no one can work. As long as I am in the world, I am the light of the world." (John 9:4,5 NKJV). Grace is the dispensation of the day, and judgment is the dispensation of the night. God is giving us the opportunity to receive His mercy now while it is day because when night comes, mercy will not be available.

"Now Enoch, the seventh from Adam, prophesied about these men also, saying, 'Behold, the LORD comes with ten thousands of His saints, to execute judgement on all, to convict all who are ungodly among them of all their ungodly deeds which they have committed in an ungodly way, and of all the harsh things which ungodly sinners have spoken against Him.'" (Jude 1:14-15 NKJV).

Jesus is KING of Kings and LORD of Lords. We have the opportunity to bow now willingly; why would we wait to bow later against our will? We have the opportunity to confess that He is LORD now willingly; why would we wait to confess He is LORD later un-willingly?

"That at the name of Jesus every knee should bow, of those in heaven, and of those on earth, and of those under the earth, and that every tongue should confess that Jesus Christ is LORD, to the glory of God the Father." (Philippians 2:10-11 NKJV).

LORD, the Kingdom is yours. You have all authority, all power, and You get all the glory forever and ever. All other governments and kingdoms are under your jurisdiction.

You are KING of Kings and LORD of Lords. We humbly submit to You, the God of grace and mercy, and the God of judgement. Because we submit to your Kingdom, we do not have to worry about the laws that govern the land; because your Kingdom will hold us to a higher standard than any kingdom or government of this world.

Heavenly father reveal to us how to surrender to You so we can receive the revelation of what we have in You. LORD encourage us and teach us how to pray. Establish our hearts so that we see you as a Father who loves us; so, we can have the confidence to approach you.

LORD help us to be confident in your Word when you said, "If you abide in Me, and my Words abide in you, you will ask what you desire, and it shall be done for you." (John 15:7 NKJV). In Jesus name we pray, Amen.

Chapter 11

The Power of Eternal Life

efore I begin to write, I ask the LORD, "How is this Word that You are about to reveal to me going to change my life and impact those who will read it?" As it pertains to a particular subject that God wants me to write about, I ask the LORD, "How do You want us to think? LORD, how do You want us to approach our lives as it pertains to this particular subject?"

Eternal life is one the most frequently asked questions as it pertains to God, spirituality, and religion. How does God want us to think as it pertains to this subject? How does God want us to view eternal life? How should we approach it? For that question to be answered, God must reveal to us how He views it.

What are God's thoughts as it pertains to eternal life? His thoughts must become our thoughts. His thoughts become our thoughts when His Word is deposited into our hearts and we allow His thoughts to reconstruct our minds.

The Bible says this, "Therefore submit to God. Resist the devil and he will flee from you." (James 4:7 NKJV). The question now becomes which God are we submitting to? Another question may be whose God are we submitting to?

Bishop Noel Jones often speaks about this, and I am paraphrasing; "No one can duplicate or imitate your concept of God. Your concept of God is yours. It has your eyes on it. It has your fingerprint. It cannot be imitated or duplicated."

Our conception of God is personal. We should never try to imitate or duplicate someone else's concept of God. Our concept of God should never be based on someone else's idea or on our own opinion. It should never be based on someone else's concept.

Our concept of God should be founded upon God's thoughts. It has to be founded upon His Word. Our relationship with God is our relationship with His Word. When we do not have a relationship with God's Thoughts, we do not have a relationship with God.

The questions now are; Are we submitting to God based on someone else's thoughts? Are we submitting to God based on our own thoughts? Or are we submitting to God based on His Thoughts?

Jesus Christ is the foundation for our relationship with God. "For no other foundation can anyone lay than that which is laid, which is Jesus Christ." (I Corinthians 3:11 NKJV). The goodness of the LORD and the mercy of God is the substratum to our relationship with Him. Our entire walk with God branches or stems out of the grace and truth that is in Christ Jesus. "For the law was given through Moses, but grace and truth came through Jesus Christ." (John 1:17 NKJV).

For years, even from childhood, we have attempted to submit to God based on someone else's idea. We have attempted to submit to God based on someone else's concept of Him. It is critical for God's Word to get on the inside of us and we get to know God for ourselves. Our concept of God will deliver us. Our concept of God will rescue us and recover us. Our concept of God will save us and make us free.

How we view God matters. Our perspective of Him matters. Our concept of God matters. When we do not believe that God is able to do it, then He will not be able to do it. When we decide that God is able to bring us out, then we will stand in the middle of our trial and declare that He is more than able.

When we believe that God is able to deliver, we stand as Hananiah, Mishael, and Azariah (also known as Shadrach, Meshach, and Abed-Nego) and declare, "O Nebuchadnezzar, we have no need to answer you in this matter. If that is the case, our God whom we serve is able to deliver us from the burning fiery furnace, and He will deliver us from your hand, O king. But If not, let it be known to you, O king, that we do not serve your gods, nor will we worship the gold image which you have set up." (Daniel 3:16b-18 NKJV).

Our God is able to deliver us and He will deliver us; but if not, we are still going to worship Him. Our God is able to deliver us and He will deliver us; but if not, we are still going to praise Him. Our

God is able to deliver us and He will deliver us; but if not, we are still going to trust Him.

"From the rising of the sun to its going down, The LORD's name is to be praised." (Psalms 113:3 NKJV). We are committed to Him in spite of the circumstance. "Though He slay me, yet will I trust Him." (Job 13:15 NKJV).

We are making a mistake when our worship and praise is predicated on or dictated by our circumstances. Circumstances fluctuate. Our God does not fluctuate. He is the same every day. God reveals to us that He is greater than our difficult circumstances. We make up in our minds that we are not going lose our worship and lose our appreciation for God by bowing down to the situation.

Our appreciation for God is not dictated by how favorable or how unfavorable our circumstances are. God is delivering us from the concept that our worship and praise is contingent upon our situations. Our worship and our praise for God is contingent upon how good and how merciful He is. He is still a good God and He is worthy to be praised.

Because we come from living a life in direct opposition to God, we sometimes fail to take responsibility for the decisions we make. As we begin to develop self-awareness and take responsibility for our decisions, we have this tendency to reinforce the condemnatory thoughts that we have towards ourselves. When we are finally introduced to God, we are introduced to a God of judgement. We attempt to submit to a God who we think is judging us when we should be submitting to a God who is saving us.

Consequently, since we are afraid of God, we are not as transparent with Him and with ourselves as we should be. Why? Because we are not going to be transparent with someone whom we are afraid of. We are only transparent with those we trust.

God wants us to know that He loves us so that we trust Him. Our deliverance and our salvation require transparency. When we trust that He loves us, we will be transparent with Him about our hurts, our issues, our flaws and our mistakes.

We will have a healthy approach to taking responsibility for what we decide to do and resist the temptation of shifting blame on others. We take responsibility for our decisions so that we can receive God's forgiveness and His cleansing. God will also give us victory in places where we use to suffer defeat.

"And if the blind leads the blind, both will fall into a ditch." (Matthew 15:14 NKJV). We get to decide who we allow to give us advice or counsel. We decide. It's our decision. When it comes to the advisors we choose, God encourages that we use discernment and not loyalty. God wants us to use discernment and not the loyalty that we have for a particular person or a particular organization when receiving advise or counsel.

"Where there is no counsel, the people fall; But in the multitude of counselors there is safety." (Proverbs 11:14 NKJV). We get to choose our counsellors. We get to choose our spiritual advisor, our legal advisor our financial advisor and our physician. We get to choose our nutritionist, our physical fitness trainer, and our cosmetologist. These are all counsellors or advisors if you will.

We want to use discernment and not loyalty when we decide which counselors, we are going to surround ourselves with because some counselors have corrupt minds. We get exploited, manipulated and/or taking advantage of by people who have corrupt minds when we are looking for results quickly. We should know what type of race we are in.

We are not in a sprint. We are in a marathon. Eternal life is a marathon. Financial success is a marathon. Weight loss is a marathon. Building a business and learning how to maintain that business is a marathon.

When we know what type of race we are in, we will prepare differently. When we know what type of race, we are in we will train accordingly. We need endurance for a marathon. We need perseverance for a marathon. We need mental resilience and intestinal fortitude for a marathon.

The race is not given to the fastest individual. Nor is it given to the strongest individual. The victory belongs to us when we endure.

We do not hit the ground running. We hit the ground crawling. We crawl until we can walk and then we walk until we can run!

We want to stay in our own lanes and not compare ourselves to others who may have been doing something for more time. When someone has been doing something for twenty-five years and we have been doing it for twenty-five minutes; well sure they may have more success than us. It's okay.

The good news is that God is no respecter of persons. If God can do it for them, then He can do it for us too. Thank you, Bishop William Murphy III for this song; God has given us the 'Same Grace'.

When we get close enough to God, we are able to discern the difference between the Spirit of Truth and the spirit of error. The spirit of error discourages the heart and causes us to move in a negative direction. The Spirit of Truth encourages the heart while causing us to move in a positive direction. The closer we get to God; the more power we have to reject something unless it is coming from the Spirit of God.

We believe with the heart that we belong to God. This belief changes how we approach our own life. God does not use intimidation to draw us. He draws us by His grace and holds us with His love.

Eternal life is a state of mind that is controlled by God's Spirit and controlled by truth. Eternal death is a state of mind controlled by satanic forces and controlled by error. The mindset that we have plays itself out in our decision making. We do not expect eternal death. We expect eternal life.

In our lives, there are two courtrooms in operation. There is the court room of public opinion and there is the court room of the Most High God. The verdict coming from the court room of public opinion is a guilty verdict. The verdict coming from court room of the Most High is a not guilty verdict. The reason why the two verdicts are different is because one court room allows us to bring our attorney and the other does not.

The court room of the Most High has jurisdiction over the court room of public opinion. We do not live our lives according to the verdict that is coming from the court of public opinion. We make decisions and live our lives predicated off the verdict that is coming from the court room of the Most High.

God is not saying that we are innocent. God is saying that we are not guilty. We are not guilty, not because we are innocent. We are not guilty because we have a Wonderful Attorney whose name is Jesus. We are not guilty because, "For unto us a Child is born, Unto us a Son is given; And the government will be upon His shoulder. And His name will be called Wonderful, Counselor, Mighty God, Everlasting Father, Prince of Peace." (Isaiah 9:6 NKJV).

We have a past. Of course, we do. Sometimes people like to bring up our past to control us or to make us feel guilty. God does not do that. We are not controlled by our past. We are controlled by the future that God has for us.

The thoughts that people think towards us can be cruel. But the thoughts that God thinks towards us are not cruel. "For I know the thoughts that I think toward you, says the LORD, thoughts of peace and not of evil, to give you a future and a hope." (Jeremiah 29:11 NKJV).

"Who shall bring a charge against God's elect? It is God who justifies." (Romans 8:33 NKJV). We have been acquitted by His blood which is validated by His own resurrection. We live as free men and free women abiding in eternal life. "Therefore if the Son makes you free, you shall be free indeed." (John 8:36 NKJV). Amen.

"Death and life are in the power of the tongue, And those who love it will eat its fruit." (Proverbs 18:21 NKJV). We should not speak other people's opinions of us. We should not speak death. We speak what God is saying about us.

We speak life. We speak life into ourselves. We speak, "And the LORD will make you the head and not the tail; you shall be above only, and not be beneath." (Deuteronomy 28:13a NKJV).

"But also for this very reason, giving all diligence, add to your faith virtue, to virtue knowledge…" (II Peter 1:5 NKJV). We always want to add to our faith. We do not want to subtract from it.

God desires for us to live a life with assurance of salvation. God wants us to live with an assurance of eternal life. When we are subtracting from our faith, by indulging in our sin-nature, we are not going to be sure that we have eternal life. Subtracting from our faith will cause a level of uncertainty.

We are going to have a very difficult time living and operating with the confidence and assurance of salvation that God desires for us when we are not adding to our faith. We the children of God add knowledge and godly character to our faith. Subtracting from our faith causes blindness to set in. Adding to our faith gives birth to revelation (vision).

"Where there is no revelation, the people cast off restraint; But happy is he who keeps the law." (Proverbs 29:18 NKJV). When we have revelation, we have vision. As simple as this may sound, having vision means being able to see. When we can see, we make better decisions.

Life is a composite of decisions. The reason we need God is because we need His help to make better decisions. God does not need us. We need Him.

We have a hunger and thirst for God that comes from Him that only He can satisfy. We have searched all over; and LORD knows we have searched all over to try to fill this hunger and thirst. We have tried to fill this thirst and hunger with all kinds of destructive things and various relationships. LORD knows we have.

What we discover is that there is nobody like Jesus. We learn that nobody can love us like the LORD. We are finding out that nothing or no one can fill this hunger and thirst but Him. "Blessed are those who hunger and thirst for righteousness, For they shall be filled." (Matthew 5:6 NKJV).

LORD help us to walk with You. As we draw closer to You, draw closer to us according to Your Word. We thank You for causing us to abound in eternal life. We live and walk with You. Father strengthen our hearts and stabilize our minds so that we may find rest in You. Thank you, LORD, for all that you do. In the name of Jesus, we pray, Amen.

Chapter 12

The Garment of Praise

　•　

The Spirit of the LORD God is upon Me, Because the LORD has anointed Me to preach good tidings to the poor; He has sent Me to heal the brokenhearted, To proclaim liberty to the captives, And the opening of the prison to those who are bound; To proclaim the acceptable year of the LORD, And the day of vengeance of our God; To comfort all who mourn, To console those who mourn in Zion, To give them beauty for ashes, The oil of joy for mourning, The garment of praise for the spirit of heaviness; That they may be called trees of righteousness, The planting of the LORD, that He may be glorified." (Isaiah 61:1-3 NKJV).

This is a very significant passage of Scripture in the life of those of us that believe. This passage of Scripture was recorded by the prophet Isaiah. In the fourth chapter of St. Luke, Jesus reads this passage of Scripture. After He reads it, He proclaims, "Today this Scripture is fulfilled in your hearing." (Luke 4:21b NKJV).

These Scriptures speak to the ministry of Christ Jesus. His ministry is a ministry of reconciliation and restoration. His ministry is a ministry of spiritual healing, psychological healing and physical healing.

When Jesus ministers to us through His Spirit, He heals our mind, and He mends our broken heart. When God speaks to us, He speaks a Word that settles our spirits and stabilizes our psyche.

Jesus did not come to the earth to condemn us. Jesus did not come to this world to judge us. Jesus came to save us. He came to give us the garment of praise (gratitude) in exchange for the spirit of heaviness (depression).

What the garment of praise suggests to us is that praise or gratitude is something that we wear internally. We can fool people with our gratitude, but we cannot fool God. "For the LORD does not see as man sees; for man looks at the outward appearance, but the LORD looks at the heart." (1 Samuel 16:7b NKJV). Praise, gratitude, or appreciation for God is totally and completely spiritual. It will be expressed externally, but it is psychological and spiritual in its connotation.

We have made the mistake in the past of seeing worship and praise as something that we do within the confines of the four walls of our local assembly. What we are finding out is that praise and worship is not just simply something we do in church. We are learning that praise and worship is a lifestyle or a way of life.

We do not need a church to praise God. We do not need a local assembly to appreciate Him. We can praise Him in our homes. We can appreciate Him while we are in our vehicles. If a global pandemic has not taught us that, then I don't know what will.

Praise means gratitude. It simply suggests thanksgiving. It has everything to do with appreciation. Appreciation for God strengthens the spiritual immune system. Being thankful guards against depression our having a heavy heart.

Jesus says this, "Come to Me, all you who labor and are heavy laden, and I will give you rest. Take My yoke upon you and learn from Me, for I am gentle and lowly in heart, and you will find rest for your souls. For My yoke is easy and My burden is light." (Matthew 11: 28-30 NKJV).

A yoke is a wooden crosspiece that is fastened over the necks of two animals and attached to the plow or cart that they are to pull. Jesus is suggesting that we take His yoke upon us and learn from Him. When we do, we will find rest or peace for our souls.

Most of us can tell when we are appreciated. We know when someone appreciates us and we know when someone is taking us for granted. Someone can try to fake their appreciation for us but sooner or later we will be able to tell if their heart is truly engaged. God is the same way and even more so because we cannot hide anything from Him.

God does not want us to fake our praise. God desires that we have authentic appreciate for Him. God does not need our praise. He wants our praise. He wants our praise because we are the ones that benefit.

God is self-sufficient and He doesn't have any needs. God is not insecure. God knows who He is. We are the ones that need to know who He is. We are the ones that need to appreciation Him. We are the ones that need to praise Him. Praise for God wars against having a heart of heaviness.

The LORD says this in the book of Isaiah, "Inasmuch as these people draw near with their mouths And honor Me with their lips, But have removed their hearts far from Me, And their fear toward Me is taught by the commandment of men." (Isaiah 29:13 NKJV).

God does not want us shouting, clapping, dancing or singing when are hearts are not engaged. God does not want us to 'praise' Him solely for the purpose of keeping up an appearance for people. God wants our appreciation for Him to be from the heart. He wants our praise to be genuine.

Our appreciation for God is dependent upon our perception of Him. It is contingent upon how we view Him, how we view ourselves, how we view others, and how we view our circumstances. What God does is He helps us to change our vantage point. It is not always about what we see but it is about how we see it. God does not always change what we see, but He will help us to change how we see it.

Two people can go through the exact same experiences. Each person as it relates to those experiences can take two totally different approaches. One person may decide to do something destruction and the other may decide to do something constructive.

A great example of this is the similarity and distinction between Judas and Peter who were two of Jesus's disciples. Both men had similar experiences who experienced different outcomes. Both men walked with Jesus. Both men had the same teacher, the same preacher, the same leader and both men made the mistake of turning their back on the LORD. One man denied Jesus and the other betrayed Him; and through it all, Jesus loved them both.

Jesus loved Judas even up to the time He was handed over to the hands of men who would ultimately have Him convicted of crimes that He did not commit and have Him sentenced to death. After all this Jesus still called Judas his friend. "Immediately he (Judas) went up to Jesus and said, 'Greetings, Rabbi!' and kissed Him. But Jesus said to him, 'Friend, why have you come?' Then they came and laid hands on Jesus and took Him." (Matthew 26:49-50 NKJV).

Jesus is never the problem. Again, Jesus is never the problem. We become the problem because we do not view Him as we should. Jesus is full of love and full of compassion. He is always extending His hand of mercy.

Peter turned His back on the LORD also. "And Peter remembered the Word of Jesus, who had said to him, Before the rooster crows, you will deny Me three times. So, he went out and wept bitterly." (Matthew 26:75 NKJV).

Both men were in the presence of the LORD daily. Both men had the same teacher and preacher. Both men were in the same environment. Both men made an egregious error. The definition of egregious is outstandingly bad or shocking. Through both of their errors, Jesus loved them both.

One man took his own life and the other man became one the world's greatest ministers of the gospel this world would ever know. What was the difference? The difference was their vantage point or point of view. It is not Who we see but how we see Him.

God sends His Word so that we see Him as always loving. He sends His Word so that we see Him as always compassionate and always gracious. God sends His Word, so we see Him as always forgiving and always extending His hand of mercy.

There is grace and mercy available for us. No matter how bad we blow it, God is right here ready to pick up the pieces. He is here to reconcile and to restore.

Jesus is near and here to mend our broken hearts and to stabilize our minds. He calls us friend even when we do not deserve to be called His friend. He gives us the garment of praise (gratitude) in exchange for the spirit of heaviness (depression).

We are not going to take our lives because we made a mistake. We are not going to take someone else's life either because things are not going our way. The devil is a lie and the truth is not in him. God is too good for us to throw our lives away. He is too good for us to give up on ourselves. Our lives are way too valuable.

God has provided an enormous sacrifice through Jesus His Son so that we may live. There is too much power in Jesus's blood and in His resurrection to let the devil have our lives. We have too much power in God to just lay down and die.

There is too much mercy and too much grace just to turn our backs on God and to turn our backs on ourselves. God loves us. He loves us. He loves us.

We are going walk with God, persevere in the race, and see what the end is going to be. We are going to watch God bring us into our purpose and into our destiny. God has brought us too far to leave us now.

"Therefore, if anyone is in Christ, he is a new creation; old things have passed away; behold, all things have become new. Now all things are of God, who has reconciled us to Himself through Jesus Christ, and has given us the ministry of reconciliation, that is, that God was in Christ reconciling the world to Himself, not imputing their trespasses to them, and has committed to us the word of reconciliation." (II Corinthians 5:17-19 NKJV).

As ministers of the gospel, appointed not by man but by God, He has given us the ministry of reconciliation. He did not give us a ministry of condemnation. God has called us to speak a Word that would reconcile His people back to Him.

It is through our own personal experiences that we learn that God is a reconciler and a restorer. We learn that God is a heart fixer from experience. We learn that God is a mind regulator though the things we go through. We learn that He is a burden barrier by what we have to endure. We learn by living that God is a heavy load sharer.

When we think of the goodness of Jesus and all that He has done for us, our soul cries out Hallelujah! We thank you LORD, for saving us. Through our experiences, God gives us the garment of praise (gratitude) in exchange for the spirit of heaviness (depression).

Our authentic appreciation for God gives us strength to minister to people. We need strength to do ministry. Not external strength but internal strength. When we lack internal strength, we allow people to 'get on our nerves'. Our praise for God is significant because our praise ushers in joy; "For the joy of the LORD is your strength." (Nehemiah 8:10 NKJV).

Ministry does not start at church. Ministry starts at home. Ministry is about helping or serving others. We make a terrible mistake and we do ourselves and others a great disservice when we are willing to do ministry at church, willing to do ministry in the streets, but not willing to do ministry at home.

We do not learn ministry in the pulpit. We learn ministry in the pew. "For if a man does not know how to rule his own house, how will he take care of the church of God." (I Timothy 3:5 NKJV).

We speak a Word of reconciliation and restoration to people when we are not condemning them. We oftentimes have condemnatory thoughts towards others because we have condemnatory thoughts towards ourselves. When we are hurting, we are condemnatory and condensing and consequently we hurt people. When we are healed, we have compassion for others and we help people.

We will find that we are most challenged when we are helping people we genuinely care about. We find this to be challenging because of the emotional investment that we have made. When we can help and serve people that we genuinely care about without losing patience, we will not have as much of a problem with helping and serving people whom we do not care about as much.

Jesus put it like this to Peter, "This is now the third time Jesus showed himself to His disciples after He was raised from the dead. So when they had eaten breakfast, Jesus said to Simon Peter, 'Simon, son of Jonah, do you love Me more than these?' He (Peter) said to Him, 'Yes, LORD; You know that I love You.' He (Jesus) said to him, 'Feed My lambs.'

"He (Jesus) said to him again a second time, 'Simon, son of Jonah, do you love Me?' He (Peter) said to Him, 'Yes, LORD; you know that I love You.' He (Jesus) said to him, 'Tend My sheep.' He (Jesus) said to him the third time, 'Simon son of Jonah do you love Me?' And he (Peter) said to him, 'LORD, You know all things, You know that I love You.' Jesus said to him, 'Feed My sheep.'" (John 21:14-17 NKJV).

There are two important messages in this passage of Scripture that God wants us to receive. The very first thing that stands out is that we must love Him. Second, we must understand people do not belong to us, but people belong to God.

When we are insecure, we can find security in managing others. When we are insecure, we can find security in managing others because it distracts us from managing ourselves. Our insecurities cause blindness as it relates to self-awareness. When we are not self-aware, we operate with a superiority complex which causes us to be condemnatory and condensing while handling others.

Consequently, we destroy our relationships with spouses, children, loved ones, family members, co-workers, business partners, and even people we attend church with.

We have to remember that people do not belong to us. Not really. God did not give us the Spirit of God to control other people. He gave us the Spirit of God so that we would control ourselves. We do not own people. We all belong to God. "The earth is the LORD's, and the fullness thereof; the world, and they that dwell therein." (Psalms 24:1 KJV).

Jesus asks us, "Do you love Me?" (John 21:16b NKJV). This critical question is asked by Jesus to all of us who not only aspire to preach or teach, but for us that also aspire to have healthy relationships. Jesus asks us this question because we have to love Him in order to handle His people properly. Without a love for Jesus we will lose patient with His people and mishandle them.

This goes for all of God's people. Not just the people who attend, participate in, and contribute financially to a local assembly. Again, "The earth is the LORD's, and the fullness thereof; the world, and they that dwell therein." (Psalms 24:1 KJV).

When we are handling people, who have behavior that is egregious and offensive, God wants us to remember that they are not rejecting us but they are rejecting Him. God has to be received. We cannot give something to someone, if they do not receive it. God does not want us losing our mind, losing our peace, and losing our joy, over wanting something for someone, when they do not want it or think they need it for themselves.

Father forgive us. Father help us especially with the people who we generally care about. Father help us with the people who we have an emotional investment with. When we do not use compassion when we handle people, and we do it in Jesus's name, we are mischaracterizing God's Word and misrepresenting His name.

Jesus uses compassion when helping others. Jesus uses patience while servings others. Our appreciation for what God has done for us will eradicate the spirit of heaviness. When we remember all the ways that God has made, and all the things that He has brought us out of; we will not operate with a spirit of heaviness. We will operate with the garment of praise.

Helping others is not about the attention or the appreciation that we receive from people. Serving others is about the appreciation and the attention that God receives. We do not take any glory for ourselves. We give God all the glory, all the honor, and all the praise that is due His name. Amen.

The Garment of Praise Part II

"And a servant of the LORD must not quarrel but be gentle to all, able to teach, patient, in humility correcting those in opposition (to themselves), if God perhaps will grant them repentance, so that they may know the truth, and that they may come to their senses and escape the snare of the devil, having been taken captive by him to do his will." (II Timothy 2:24-26 NKJV).

If you have not had the opportunity to watch Bishop Noel Jones's teaching entitled "Preaching 101", I strongly suggest and I highly recommend doing so. This teaching is not just for those of us who aspire to preach and teach the gospel; there are principles taught in this lesson that can be applied to daily life. I strongly suggest taking a look at it.

In this lesson, Bishop Noel Jones discusses the use of an instrument or a tool that is familiar to all of us. That instrument would happen to be a knife. I will attempt to paraphrase and/or "piggy back" if you will, off of what was taught in this lesson.

"For the Word of God is living and powerful, and sharper than any two-edged sword, piercing even to the division of soul and spirit, and of joints and marrow, and is a discerner of the thoughts and intents of the heart." (Hebrews 4:12 NKJV). The Word of God is referred to in various passages of Scriptures as a sword. Knives are more common today than swords so for the purposes of this conversation let's call the Word of God a knife.

A knife is an instrument that can be used correctly and it can also be used incorrectly. We can take a knife and stab someone with it, injuring them and causing great bodily harm. We can also take that same instrument and preform a surgery and help them to heal.

The Scriptures are an instrument. The Scriptures are a knife. The Scriptures can be used correctly and unfortunately, they can also be used incorrectly. A very subtle question to ask before moving forward. Have we ever stabbed someone or been stabbed by someone with Scripture? For most of us the answer to this question is yes.

Jesus does not use the Scriptures to injure us. He is a physician. He is a surgeon. He is not a mugger. Jesus uses Scripture to perform surgery and to help us to heal. When we are being stabbed with Scriptures, or when we are stabbing others with Scriptures, the Scriptures are being used incorrectly.

We do not need patience to stab someone; but we do however need patience to perform surgery. Gentleness is not required to stab someone; but gentleness is required to perform surgery. We do not need compassion to stab someone; but we do need compassion to perform surgery.

None of us want or need a surgeon who does not have these three characteristics. We most definitely want and need a surgeon with patience, gentleness and compassion. When these characteristics are a part of our character, we are equipped and can be used as instruments in God's hand to perform surgery on others.

We sometimes take it personal when someone whom we really care about has dysfunctional thinking that is leading to destructive behavior. It is very challenging to watch someone that we care about remain in a perpetual state of destruction. This can be heart wrenching, frustrating, and grueling, to say the least.

In the text mentioned at the beginning of this chapter, Paul says, "in humility correcting those in opposition (to themselves)." (II Timothy 2:25a NKJV). Our frustration stems from making the mistake of seeing people with dysfunctional thinking and destructive behavior as being in opposition to us. When people have dysfunctional thinking and destructive behavior, they are not in opposition to us. They are in opposition to themselves.

How can someone be hurting us when, "No weapon formed against (us) shall prosper." (Isaiah 54:17a NKJV). How can someone be hurting us when, "All things work together for good to those who love God, to those who are the called according to His purpose." (Romans 8:28 NKJV). How can someone be hurting us when, "Weeping may endure for a night, But joy comes in the morning." (Psalms 30:5 NKJV).

God gives us the garment of praise (gratitude), in exchange for the spirit of heaviness (depression) so that we can view people as not hurting us, but as hurting themselves. When we see people as hurting us, we move with bitterness, anger and cruelty. When we see people as hurting themselves, we operate with patience, gentleness, and compassion.

Compassion is where we are able to feel what someone is feeling. When we are helping people who are in opposition to themselves, God wants us to use mercy. God does not want us to feel sorry for people. He wants us to feel what others are feeling.

God has compassion for us. The Bible says that, "For we do not have a High Priest who cannot sympathize with our weaknesses, but was in all points tempted as we are, yet without sin." (Hebrews 4:15 NKJV). Jesus does not feel sorry for us. He has compassion for us. God feels what we are feeling.

God will feel what we are feeling but He will not feel sorry for us because, "As His divine power has given to us all things that pertain to life and godliness through the knowledge of Him." (II Peter 1:3 NKJV). When we are going through with adverse circumstances or with negative people we have a tendency to throw pity parties. We throw pity parties, send out invitations, and look for people to attend.

We not only send out invitations to our pity parties to people, we also send out invitations to God. God refuses to attend our pity party because pity enables us to be dysfunctional and destructive to self and others. God does not attend our pity party because he is only interested in empowering us.

When we get ready to throw a party and we need God to attend, we should not throw a pity; we should throw a praise party because as Bishop Noel Jones said, "God does not dwell in the midst of our pity, He dwells in the midst of our praise." So that we can get the victory in our situation, God will give us a Word that will give us the garment of praise in exchange for the spirit of heaviness.

Using our experiences of what God has done in our lives will empowers us to speak a Word of healing into someone's life. Impure motives and personal agendas pertaining to ministering to people lead to bad decision making. Remembering what it feels like to be in a low place can give us the patience we need to handle the people that we find to be challenging.

"My brethren, let not many of you become teachers, knowing that we shall receive a stricter judgment." (James 3:1 NKJV). Those of us that are ministers of the Gospel are held to a higher standard. "For everyone to whom much is given, from him much will be required." (Luke 12:48 NKJV). This is something that we should accept before we answer the call to ministry.

We should have a relationship with the LORD before we attempt to minister to people. We will injure ourselves and we will injure people when we do not know God for ourselves. Unfortunately, sometimes we think we know Him and we don't.

Some of us enjoy watching the National Basketball Association (NBA). Some of us are huge fans. What a lot of the players and coaches in the NBA are not fans of, are their media obligations. They are not huge fans of their media obligations because their words often times get taken out of context.

Many times, we hear a quote of what a player or a coach said, but sometimes we do not always hear the context in which they said it. This opens the door for mischaracterizations of their words thereby causing their names to be misrepresented. Now, if we as people do not enjoy having our words taken out of context, which leads to a mischaracterization and a misrepresentation of our name, how much more God.

Scripture is not really intended to be read like text messages. Scripture is intended to be read more like emails. Chapter and verse were not added to the Scriptures by the original author. Chapter and verse were added to the Scriptures later to help us bookmark the Scriptures and to help us navigate through the Bible.

When handling God's Word, our motivation should not be to manipulate, exploit or to control others. This makes people think and feel more negatively of themselves than they already do. Always, when handling God's Word, our motivation has to be reconciliation and restoration. When we use the Word to empower ourselves, we will then use the Word to empower others.

"Beloved, do not believe every spirit, but test the spirits, whether they are of God; because many false prophets have gone out into the world." (I John 4:1 NKJV). We discussed this in an earlier chapter but because of the day and time we live in, this cannot be said enough. We must use discernment when receiving messages.

Receiving messages from individuals who are condescending and condemnatory will rob us of our joy and discourage us. We cannot better ourselves when we are discouraged. For us to better ourselves we have to be encouraged. We do not want to receive messages from people who have a spirit of heaviness. We want to receive truth from people who have the garment of praise.

Because there are so many fraudulent prophets and false teachers, it is critical that we discern truth from error. The last thing we want or need to do is follow someone into a ditch or lead someone into one because we cannot see. "And if the blind lead the blind, both will fall into a ditch." (Matthew 15:14b NKJV).

All of us are not called to preach and teach the Gospel. That's okay. Nothing is wrong with that. When we discover ourselves in God, we will learn what our gifts and talents are. We will also find our passion and what God has placed us on this earth to do.

Walking in someone else's calling or walking in someone else's purpose for our lives produces a spirit of heaviness. Walking in the calling and purpose of God produces a spirit of praise. God is not calling us to a spirit of heaviness. God is calling us to put on the garment of praise.

When God calls us to do something, He will give us the gift and the talent to do it. He will also give us the passion to do it. Many times, our problem is not our gift, our talent, or our passion. Many times, our problem is the deficiencies in our character.

Gifts are given. Character has to develop. We do not always have the character necessary to support what God has gifted us to do. Our gift will take us there, but when we do not have character, we find ourselves right back where we started. What we want to do, so that our character develops is, "Wait on the LORD; Be of good courage, And He shall strengthen our heart; Wait, I say, on the LORD!" (Psalms 27:14 NKJV).

What we do not want, and what we surely do not need is to find ourselves in a situation where we get to the end of our lives and at the beginning of eternity and we have this dialogue with Jesus: "Many will say to Me in that day, 'LORD, LORD, have we not prophesied in Your name, cast out demons in Your name, and done many wonders in Your name?' And then I will declare to them, "I never knew you; depart from Me, you who practice lawlessness!'" (Matthew 7:22-23 NKJV).

When we read this passage of Scripture, it is easy to miss what's going on in the text. What we should pay attention to is the arrogance displayed by these individuals that were standing before the LORD. Right now Jesus is sitting on a Throne of Grace. Later He will be sitting on a Throne of Judgement. Teaching, preaching and prophesying cannot save us.

When we are standing before God, this is not the time to go over our resume. This is the time to ask for mercy. Our resumes' cannot save us. Our resume cannot wash away our sins. 'What can wash away our sins? Nothing but the Blood of Jesus. What can make us whole again? Nothing but the Blood of Jesus.'

Jesus declares in this passage of Scripture, "I never knew you." (Matthew 7:23b NKJV). They didn't know Him. We do not go over our resume when we are standing before God when we know Him. When we are standing before Him, and we know Him, we ask for mercy.

We want to know Jesus now while He is sitting on a Throne of Grace. We do not want to have to wait to try to get to know Him later while He is sitting on a Throne of Judgement. When we know Him, He removes the fear of judgement because mercy triumphs over judgement. Our God removes the fear of condemnation and gives us the garment of praise (appreciation) for salvation, in exchange for the spirit of heaviness (depression) that comes with the fear of judgement.

Paul says this to those of us that desire to oversee God's work and watch over His people: "Not a novice, lest being puffed up with pride he fall into the same condemnation as the devil." (I Timothy 3:6 NKJV).

In this particular text Paul goes through a list of qualifications that an individual who desires the work of an overseer should have. After going through the list, He says that He should not be a novice. The word novice means inexperienced.

A lot of times when we go for a job, we are not qualified for the job because of lapses in our work history or a lack of experience. This can be frustrating because what we say is 'How can we get experience if we never get an opportunity?' Here Paul is not talking about experience with ministry or work experience. Paul is talking about experience with God.

It is not experience with teaching, preaching and/or prophesying that qualifies us to do ministry. It is experience with God and navigating through personal difficulty that qualifies us. We experience God in our personal lives and convey those experiences to others.

Asking God respectfully, 'What do You want from me?', sometimes causes hesitation on our part because we may be afraid that He may ask us to give up something that we are not ready to let go of. We have grown accustom to telling the LORD what we want or asking Him for what we thought we needed. Our question now is, 'LORD, what do You want from me?'; and the other question is, 'LORD, what do I need?'

May the LORD help us to not put more on ourselves than what we can bear. May the LORD help us to not allow others to put more on us than what we can bear. Our God will never put more on us than what we can bear. May the LORD give us the garment of praise in exchange for the spirit of heaviness.

While we have breath in our body and while God's grace and mercy is available, we pray; "So teach us to number our days, that we gain a heart of wisdom." (Psalms 90:12 NKJV) . Yesterday is covered by God's mercy and tomorrow is not promised. LORD help us to praise and worship You while we have this opportunity.

"Therefore do not worry about tomorrow, for tomorrow will worry about its own things. Sufficient for the day is its own trouble." (Matthew 6:34 NKJV). Father deliver us from procrastination. Deliver us from prolonging our deliverance and from extending our stay in our wilderness.

Father deliver us from worrying about tomorrow. We will praise You for helping us to get through today. "This is the day the LORD has made; We will rejoice and be glad in it." (Psalms 118:24 NKJV).

Father we will remember the exhortation that says, "I can do all things through Christ who strengthens me." (Philippians 4:13 NKJV). We thank You Father for Your goodness and for Your mercy towards us. We love You and we are forever grateful. We give you all the glory, all the honor, and all the praise that's due Your name. In the name of Jesus, we pray, Amen.

References

---

1. You Version, (Bible.com), http://bible.com/1/pro. KJV, NKJV, AMP, NASB.

2. Oxford Languages Dictionary provided by Google (Oxford: Oxford University Press, 2020), http://OxfordDictionaries.com.

About Author

Who is Jerome W. Terry? Jerome is an heir of God and a joint heir with Christ Jesus. He is someone who does not define himself by what he does. He defines himself by who is in God.

Jerome encourages and teaches renewal of the mind from a Christian point-of-view so that we may better ourselves and strengthen our relationship with God. He uses his experiences and couples them with the Word to help people with their lives.

Jerome W. Terry writes and speaks with a unique perspective. His unique perspective does not come from a pulpit. Jerome's unique perspective comes from a pew. Because of his unique perspective, he has an uncommon ability to empathize with people's pain and with what they may be feeling.

Jerome is able to provide a voice of inspiration those who may be wrestling with some of the many things that he has had to overcome. He offers encouragement and teaching to believers who desire to be transformed by the renewing of the mind. To learn more, please visit www.jeromewterry.com

Pure Thoughts Publishing LLC